*Richard Musman*

D1828321

# Read all about it!

*Longman*

## ACKNOWLEDGMENTS

We would like to thank the following for permission to reproduce the illustrations:

George W. Abel for p. 9, bottom; The Princess Alexandra Hospital, Harlow for p. 107, top; The Arthur Murray School of Dancing for p. 47, bottom; The Baltic Exchange for p. 29, top; Barnaby's Picture Library for p. 1; 5, top; 31; 43, bottom; 77; 91; 95, top; 99, bottom; 103, top; British European Airways for p. 25; The British Tourist Authority for p. 121; The British Printer and Strachan and Henshaw Ltd. for p. 73, bottom; The Central Electricity Generating Board for p. 89, top; The Commissioner of the Metropolitan Police for p. 103, bottom; Cornelsen-Velhagen and Klasing for p. 9, bottom; Dickins and Jones for p. 81, bottom; The English Country Cheese Council for p. 51, top; Ford Motor Company for p. 17; The General Post Office for p. 65, top; 119, bottom; 122; Richard Hamnett for p. 5, bottom; 39; 111, bottom; The Inner London Education Authority, College for the Distributive Trades for p. 81, top; Peter Lane for p. 35; 69, top; 85, bottom; 115, bottom; Midland Bank Ltd. for p. 119, top; The Ministry of Transport for p. 43, top; The Pitman School of English for p. 9, top; Paul Popper for p. 21; 47, top; 55, bottom; 65, bottom; 69, bottom; 89, bottom; 111, top; The P. & O. Line for p. 13, bottom; The Radio Times Hulton Picture Library for p. 85, top; Road Research Laboratory for p. 95, bottom; The Royal Society for the Prevention of Accidents for p. 99, top; The Times for p. 73, top; Topix for p. 13, top; 107, bottom; Trust Houses Ltd. for the Star Inn, Alfriston, p. 115, top; The Westmorland Gazette for p. 59, bottom; Wiltshire Newspapers for p. 55, top; The Youth Hostels Association for p. 59, top.

LONGMAN GROUP LIMITED
London
*Associated companies, branches and representatives throughout the World*

© Longman Group Ltd 1971
All rights reserved. No part of this publication may be reproduced, stored in a retrieval system or transmitted in any form or by any means—electronic, mechanical, photocopying, recording, or otherwise—without the prior permission of the copyright owner.

*First published 1971*
*New impressions *1972; *1973 (twice); *1974; *1975; *1976*
ISBN 0 582 52542 x
*Printed in Hong Kong by Dai Nippon Printing Co (H.K.) Ltd*

# Contents


**1** WORK FOR A VISITOR TO BRITAIN

1:1 **Arrival in Britain** page 2
1:2 **Au Pair** 6
1:3 **A Hotel Waiter** 10
1:4 **A Garage Mechanic** 14
1:5 **A Hospital Nurse** 18
1:6 **An Airport Reception Clerk** 22
1:7 **An Exporter's Secretary** 26

**2** FREE TIME AND HOLIDAYS

2:1 **A Quiet Evening Out** 32
2:2 **Week-end Shopping** 36
2:3 **Amateur Mechanics** 40
2:4 **Dancing** 44
2:5 **Parties** 48
2:6 **Watching Football** 52
2:7 **A Holiday in the Lake District** 56

**3** A FIRST JOB

3:1 **At the Post Office** 62
3:2 **At the Hairdresser's** 66
3:3 **At the Printer's** 70
3:4 **A Photographic Shop** 74
3:5 **Window-dressing** 78
3:6 **In the Office** 82
3:7 **An Electrician** 86

**4** THEY SERVE THE PUBLIC

4:1 **Accident** 92
4:2 **Fire** 96
4:3 **Police** 100
4:4 **Hospital** 104
4:5 **Travelling** 108
4:6 **Hotels** 112
4:7 **Money Matters** 116
**Appendix** 120

# I

## WORK FOR A VISITOR TO BRITAIN

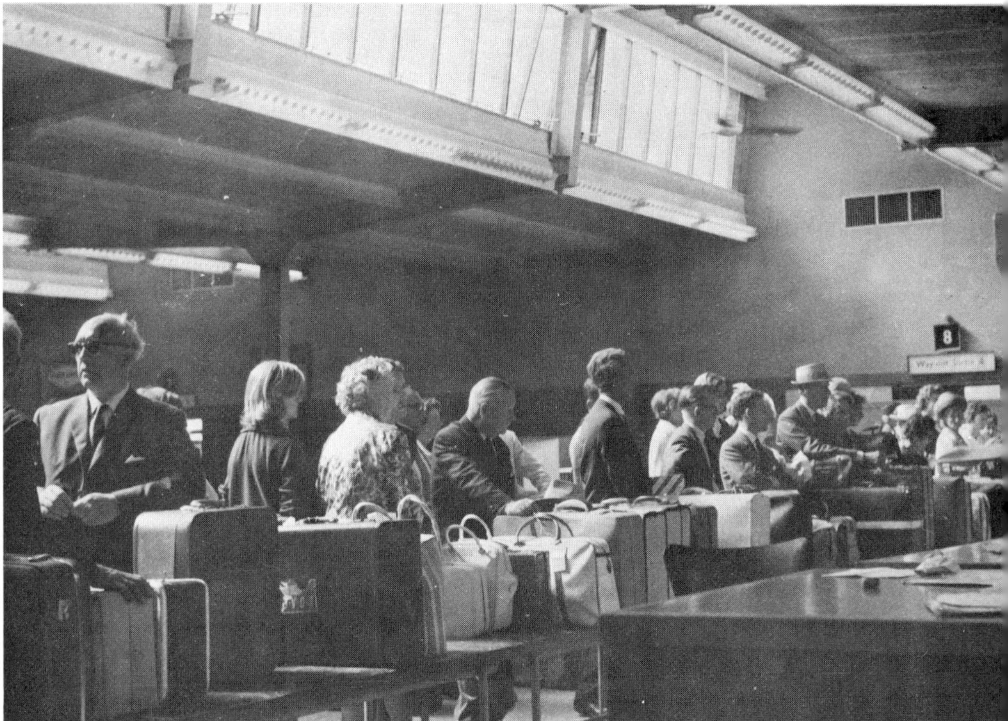

# 1:1 Arrival in Britain

**accent** /'æksənt/ speech sounds that are different from the "usual" sounds of English. *She has a strong Scottish accent. He is French but he speaks English without an accent.*

**bacon** /'beikən/ salty preserved meat from the side or back of a pig. *Nobody can explain the British love of bacon and fried eggs for breakfast.*

**blanket** /'blæŋkit/ square piece of warm cloth for a bed. *He likes three blankets on his bed in winter.*

**boat train** /'bəut trein/ special train to take people to or from a ship. *The boat train from Dover reaches London in 1½ hours.*

**carriage** /'kæridʒ/ part of a train with seats for about eighty people. *There were eight carriages on the train—one 1st class carriage and seven 2nd class carriages.*

**cornflakes** /'kɔːnfleiks/ thin pieces of rolled cooked corn. *You eat cornflakes for breakfast with milk and sugar.*

**escalator** /'eskəleitə/ moving stairs to carry people up and down to the different floors of a big shop or the Underground. *Old ladies are sometimes afraid to step on or off the escalator.*

**journey** /'dʒəːni/ travelling from one place to another. *We had a good journey by train and ship from London to Paris. The journey to Kabul by road is a difficult one.*

**landlady** /'lænleidi/ woman who owns a house; other people pay to live in her house. *Paul's landlady gives him breakfast but no other meals.*

**luggage** /'lʌgidʒ/ a traveller's bags and suitcases. *We'll put our luggage in the left-luggage office while we look round the town.*

**permit** /'pəːmit/ paper to show that the government allows you to do something. *If you are not British, you need a work permit to earn money in Britain.*

**platform** /'plætfɔːm/ part of a station where trains arrive or leave. *In British stations the platforms are 3 feet (1 m.) above the lines. The train from Dover arrives at Platform 6.*

**toast** /təust/ pieces of bread made brown by fire. *Grandmother made toast in front of the fire, but we use an electric toaster.*

**would rather** /wud 'rɑːðə/ prefer. *"Would you rather have tea or coffee?"—"I'd rather have tea."*

## "Just make yourself at home"

LANDLADY Good morning, Paul. You're up early. Did you sleep well?
PAUL Very well indeed, thank you, Mrs Sprigg. English beds are wonderful!
LANDLADY Are you sure you've got enough blankets?
PAUL Quite sure, thank you. I was very warm.
LANDLADY That's good. Now what would you like for breakfast? Cornflakes? Eggs and bacon? Toast?
PAUL Just toast, please. I'm not very hungry this morning.
LANDLADY Of course you're not! You must still be tired after your journey. Sit down at the table and I'll bring you a nice cup of tea. Or would you rather have coffee?
PAUL Tea, please. I drink coffee at home, but I'd rather drink tea in England.
LANDLADY You speak English very well. Where did you learn it?
PAUL I learned it at school.
LANDLADY Well, ask when you don't understand things.
PAUL You're very kind, Mrs Sprigg.
LANDLADY Not at all. Just make yourself at home.
PAUL I think I'll have eggs and bacon after all.
LANDLADY Would you like cornflakes first?
PAUL No, thank you, not today. But tomorrow, perhaps.

---

## Exercise

1 *Example* You don't understand? Ask.
*Answer* Ask when you don't understand.

1 You are hungry? Have some eggs and bacon.
2 You are cold? Use another blanket.
3 You are lonely? Talk to the landlady.
4 You're in a hurry? Go by Underground.
5 You're ready for breakfast? Have some cornflakes.
6 You want to go to France? Take your passport.

2 *Example* "I'm not very hungry," said Paul.
*Answer* Paul said that he wasn't very hungry.

1 English beds are wonderful.
2 I drink coffee at home.
3 I'd rather drink tea in England.
4 I learned English at school.
5 I'll have eggs and bacon after all.
6 I need a work permit.

## Nothing to declare

Paul was standing in the front of the boat. He was looking towards England. The coast got nearer and nearer. "I'll soon be there!" he thought. He was just going to pick up his luggage when he remembered his passport. He ran at once to the passport office. A tall, dark-haired girl was standing in front of him. "Well!" Paul thought. "I hope that all English girls look like her!"

When the boat reached Dover he went up to her at the Customs. Both her cases were open and the Customs officer was looking in every corner. The girl saw Paul and smiled. Then she shut her cases and walked towards the boat train.

Paul put his own cases in front of the Customs officer. He was still watching the girl. "I have nothing to declare," he said quickly, "and I have no work permit. I am only staying in England for two months." The Customs officer laughed and marked Paul's two cases with a piece of white chalk. "If you hurry," he said, "you may catch her!"

Paul ran on to the platform, but he could not see the girl. He walked along the train. At last he saw a head of dark hair at a window. He climbed quickly into the carriage and sat down in the next seat. But he had made a mistake. His neighbour was a long-haired boy.

Two hours later the train reached Victoria Station. Paul had already forgotten about the girl. He was now thinking about his new landlady. Her name was Mrs Sprigg and she lived in Edgware in the north of London. Mrs Sprigg was a friend of his mother's. He was going to stay with her while he studied English at a London college.

Edgware was a long way from Victoria. A policeman told him that it was on the Underground. "Don't forget to change at Charing Cross," warned the policeman.

At Charing Cross there were so many passages and escalators that Paul soon lost his way. But at last he reached the Edgware Line platform. It was full of people. A train came in at once. The doors opened. Everybody rushed forward. Paul found an empty seat and sat down. He soon fell asleep.

"Wake up!" somebody said suddenly. "This is the end of the line." Paul opened his eyes. It was the pretty girl. "Hello!" he cried.

"I was passing your carriage, and I noticed that you were asleep," the girl said. "So ——"

"Do you live in Edgware too?" cried Paul. "That's nice!"

"Edgware?" she said. "Is that where you want to go? Then you've come the wrong way. This is Morden—the other end of the line."

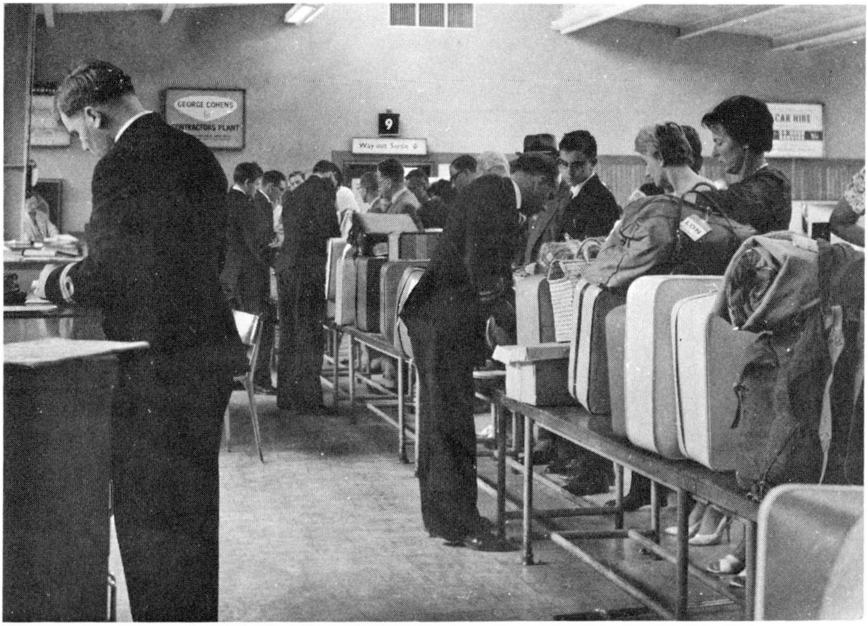


After the visitor arrives in Britain he must go to the Customs Shed. His luggage is soon checked and the visitor can begin his stay.

Small hotels in Britain give an English breakfast to all guests, but do not always give lunch or an evening meal. Bed and breakfast costs about £1 in small towns and £2 in big cities. Big hotels cost much more.

# 1:2 Au Pair

**au pair** /əu 'pɛə/ (French) An "au pair" works in the house while she learns English. She lives as a member of the family. *Our "au pair" girl is free every afternoon and spends two hours at a language school.*

**busy** /'bizi/ with very many things to do. *I've had a busy day, and I'm tired.*

**dining-room** /'dainiŋrum/ room with a large table for meals. *The kitchen is usually near the dining-room.*

**dish-water** /'diʃwɔːtə/ water that has been used for *washing up* (see below). *If the tea looks like dish-water, we don't drink it.*

**homework** /'həumwəːk/ work that the teacher asks us to do at home. *I've got too much homework, so I can't come to the cinema with you.*

**let's** /lets/ I think that it would be good to (do something). *Let's play some records. Let's hope that he will soon be better.*

**make the beds** /'meik ðə 'bedz/ put the bedclothes on the beds and make them tidy. *She always makes the beds after she has done the shopping.*

**mind** /maind/ not like (something), be displeased about. *Do you mind if I smoke? I don't mind washing up.*

**peel** /piːl/ take the outer skin off fruit etc. *Please peel an orange for me, but don't throw the peel on the grass.*

**record** /'rekɔːd/ —if you want to hear music at home, you can turn on the radio or listen to a *record. You put the record on a record-player. After you have listened to it, you turn the record-player off.*

**sofa** /'səufə/ seat for two or three people in a living-room. *When I was ill, they made up a bed for me on the sofa.*

**thief** /θiːf/ person who steals things. *A thief took my bag out of the car. We lock up our houses for fear of thieves.*

**wash up** /'wɔʃ 'ʌp/ wash the plates, knives and forks etc. after a meal. *I'll help you to wash up and then we'll go out. We'll do the washing-up first.*

**I'm afraid** You say this to prepare somebody for bad news. *I'm afraid (that) I've broken your camera. I'm afraid you can't have the car this afternoon.*

## A cup of tea

VISITOR Is Mrs Lodge in? I'm Mrs Clegg.

LILI I'm afraid Mrs Lodge is out. But she'll be here soon. Would you like to wait? I'm the "au pair" girl. Please come in.

MRS CLEGG Well, just for a few moments, then.

LILI I've just made a pot of tea. Would you like a cup?

MRS CLEGG I'd love one. It's such a hot day.

LILI Would you like some cake with your tea?

MRS CLEGG Oh no, thank you! And don't put any sugar in my tea. I'm getting too fat.

LILI You're not fat at all. Please sit down. I'll bring your tea at once.

MRS CLEGG You are a kind girl. (*She looks at the tea*) Is this the tea?

LILI Yes. I hope you like it.

MRS CLEGG (*She tastes the tea*) I've never tasted such nice tea, but do you mind if I tell you something, my dear?

LILI Of course not.

MRS CLEGG Well, we always make tea with *boiling* water. This tea tastes very nice, but it looks rather like dish-water, doesn't it?

---

## Exercise

1 *Example* This is very nice tea (taste)
*Answer* This tea tastes very nice.

1 This is very nasty dish-water. (look)
2 These are very nice potatoes. (taste)
3 This is very difficult homework. (seem)
4 This is a very big dining-room. (look)
5 This is very hot washing-up water. (feel)
6 This is a very dirty living-room. (smell)

2 *Example* They have a plan for tonight—to go to a party.
*Answer* They are going to a party tonight.

1 Lili has a plan for tonight—to play records.
2 She has a plan for tomorrow—to visit the Tower of London.
3 They have a plan for next week—to fly to Paris.
4 I have a plan for this evening—to go to the pictures.
5 Mrs Lodge has a plan for tomorrow—to mend the teapot.
6 We have a plan for next Thursday—to come here.

## "Please don't!"

It was nearly 6 o'clock. Lili went into the living-room and sat down on the sofa. She was tired. She had had a busy day. She had cooked breakfast for Mr and Mrs Lodge and their four children. She had washed up all the plates and cups and had broken the teapot. Then she had made all the beds and peeled a lot of potatoes. In the afternoon she had spent two hours at the language school and had walked home in the rain. She picked up a newspaper. "AU PAIR GIRL SAVES FAMILY JEWELS FROM THIEF", she read. "It would be nice to have my name in the newspapers!" she thought.

At that moment the door opened and Nick walked in. Nick was nineteen, and the oldest of the Lodge children. He was tall, dark and good-looking. "Hello, Lili!" he said. "Are you all alone? Mother and Father are going to a party tonight. We'll play records together, if you like."

"That would be lovely," Lili said.

She and Nick and Jane, the thirteen-year-old daughter, had supper together in the kitchen. They enjoyed it very much. After supper, Jane took her homework into the dining-room. Nick and Lili went into the living-room. They sat down on the sofa together. Nick put on his new jazz records. Lili was happy.

Suddenly there was a loud knock on the front door. Lili looked at the clock. It was 12.30. "It's very late," she said. "Who is it?"

"I don't know," said Nick. "Wait here. I'll go to the door."

Lili turned off the record-player and listened. Somebody was shouting. She ran into the hall. A large man was standing on the steps. He was waving his arms. It was Bob Parfitt, the neighbour. "Why are you making all that noise?" he shouted.

Bob Parfitt was big and strong and he loved a fight. Everybody in the street was afraid of him. Lili was frightened. She was sure that he was going to hit Nick. She rushed between them. "Please don't!" she cried.

Bob Parfitt was surprised. He stepped back, fell down the steps and hit his head on a stone. At that moment a policeman passed. He stopped and picked Bob Parfitt up. "Are you all right, sir?" he asked Bob.

But Bob could not answer and the policeman had to call a doctor. Bob was still unable to talk when the doctor arrived. So the doctor sent him to hospital. Meanwhile the policeman asked Nick and Lili a few questions.

"You'll have to come with me," he said, "and let's hope that Mr Parfitt is able to talk in the morning."

Bob Parfitt was able to talk in the morning. So Lili had her name in the newspapers. "AU PAIR GIRL KNOCKS OUT NEIGHBOUR. SHE AND BOY-FRIEND SPEND NIGHT AT POLICE STATION."

An au pair girl lives with a family and helps in the house. In the afternoon or evening she usually goes to a language school. Some of the language schools in London teach English by the most modern methods. In her English language class she will meet visitors to Britain from many different countries.

Some au pairs like to work with a family in the country. Of course they will not meet other foreigners. But they will meet more British people. Life in an English village is very friendly.

# 1:3 A Hotel Waiter

**all right** /ˈɔːl ˈrait/ I agree. *"Let's go to the Starlight Coffee Bar."—"All right."*

**bar** /bɑː/ high narrow table for drinks, or the room that it is in. *He's standing at the bar, having a gin and orange.*

**cheque** /tʃek/ an order to pay money. *You paid me by cheque, but your bank won't give me the money—you forgot to sign your cheque.*

**choose** /tʃuːz/ decide to have one thing and not another. *When you choose, you make a choice. Mary chose fried fish, but my choice was an omelette.*

**course** /kɔːs/ one part of a meal. *We had a four-course meal; the courses were: soup, fish, roast and sweet or cheese.*

**foreign** /ˈfɔrin/ of or from another country. *When we go to a foreign country, we are foreigners in that country.*

**madam** /ˈmædəm/ polite word to use when one speaks to a lady. *Please come this way, madam. Will you have some more coffee, madam?*

**manager** /ˈmænidʒə/ head man in a hotel, shop etc. *I am very angry and I want to see the hotel manager at once.*

**menu** /ˈmenjuː/ list of dishes that a restaurant will serve. *I'm afraid baked apples aren't on the menu today, sir.*

**order** (v.) /ˈɔːdə/ tell somebody to do something; tell a waiter to bring something. *He ordered a glass of wine.*

**restaurant** /ˈrestrɔnt/ large room for meals in a hotel etc. *The ship has four restaurants.*

**tip** /tip/ present of money in return for good service. *In a restaurant we add a tip of ten to fifteen per cent if there is no service charge. I tipped the bell-boy.*

**I'd love to** Yes, I'd like (to do) that very much. *'Will you have dinner with us next Saturday?"—"I'd love to! I'd love to see your new baby."*

**Leave it to me** I'll look after everything, so don't worry. *"Your car isn't running well, sir? Leave it to me."*

## "Waiter!"

MAN Waiter! I saw you drop this knife on the floor. It's dirty.
CHRISTIAN I'm sorry, sir. I'll bring you another one.
SECOND MAN Waiter! This soup is cold, and there's too much salt in it.
CHRISTIAN I'll take it back to the kitchen, sir. Would you mind ——
THIRD MAN Waiter! This water is warm. Bring me some ice.
CHRISTIAN Yes, sir, but—
THIRD MAN I've waited long enough! Get me the manager!
CHRISTIAN (*to the manager*) Excuse me, sir. This gentleman ——
MANAGER Don't worry me now, boy. I'm busy. Serve those ladies over there. They're in a hurry.
CHRISTIAN (*to waitress*) What shall I do? I can't serve everybody at the same time.
WAITRESS Leave it to me. You serve the ladies. I'll look after the men.
CHRISTIAN You're very kind. Are you free tomorrow evening?
WAITRESS Yes. Why?
CHRISTIAN Will you come out with me?
WAITRESS I'd love to. Where?
CHRISTIAN Well, you know the town, and I don't. So you'd better choose.
WAITRESS All right. We'll go to Antonio's. It's a coffee bar, and they don't have waiters there!

---

## Exercise

**1** *Example* You dropped the knife. I saw you.
*Answer* I saw you drop the knife.

1 You tipped the waitress. I saw you.
2 He called the manager. We heard him.
3 She ordered a five-course dinner. He heard her.
4 You destroyed the menu. I watched you.
5 The foreigner chose a good wine. They heard him.
6 I called her madam. You heard me.

**2** *Example* You know the town. I'm different.
*Answer* You know the town, and I don't.

1 They like coffee. He's different.
2 We eat bacon and eggs. She's different.
3 I like red wine. You're different.
4 Paul eats cornflakes. I'm different.
5 He wants cream in his coffee. They're different.
6 You like ice in your drink. Paul's different.

## A table for two

Christian was working in a restaurant on the London road. One day he looked out of the window and saw an old Rolls Royce in the car park. A very fat lady in a fur coat got out and came into the restaurant. She had with her a small fat dog.

"A table for two," she said to Christian.

"This way, madam," said Christian. He was very pleased. "Ladies like that usually give good tips," he thought. He handed her the menu.

"Would you like to order now, madam," he said, "or will you wait for your friend?"

"Friend?" said the woman. She seemed to be surprised. "I'm alone. The other place is for my dog." At that moment the dog jumped on to the empty chair and sat down. The woman looked at the menu. She ordered a five-course lunch—soup, fish, chicken and rice, fruit with cream, and cheese. She also ordered a bottle of the most expensive French wine.

"And the dog, madam?" Christian began.

"Fido?" answered the woman. "Fido always sits at table with me."

When Christian told the manager about Fido, he laughed. "We sometimes get women like that," he said. "Serve the lady and don't worry about the dog."

Christian served the lady. While she ate she gave little pieces of fish and meat to Fido. Fido ate them and asked for more.

"Oh dear!" said the lady. "I've given so much chicken to Fido that I'm still hungry. Please bring me some roast duck."

Christian brought the roast duck and the lady gave a lot of that to Fido too. Then when she had finished the meal she ordered coffee and a large box of the most expensive cigarettes. "A very nice meal," she said at last. "Now will you please bring me my bill."

Christian added up the bill. It came to £3. The woman looked at the bill. Then she looked at Christian.

"You're foreign, aren't you?" she asked.

"Yes, madam," answered Christian.

"Hmm. £3. That's a lot of money. I'll have to pay by cheque."

The woman signed the cheque and Christian took it straight to the manager's office.

"Tell her—politely—that we don't accept cheques," said the manager. But it was too late. The woman had gone. The manager telephoned the bank at once, but the bank had never heard of the woman! The manager was very angry.

"Excuse me, sir," said Christian. "But I can remember the number of the car. It was CHR 17. You see, I'm 17 years old and my name——"

The manager picked up the telephone again. "Give me the police station," he said.

Half an hour later the manager called Christian. He was laughing.

"They've caught her," he said. "And Fido was still hungry! He bit a policeman."

Today waiters and chefs can train for their jobs at technical colleges. In this restaurant in a college, lunch is served to the public. Students cook the food and serve it. Businessmen and housewives go to this restaurant because it is cheap and the food is very good.

Tea on a modern ship is a meal like supper on land. There are many different dishes and many waiters to serve them.

# 1:4 A Garage Mechanic

**carburettor** /ˈkɑːbjuretə/ part of a petrol engine; it mixes petrol and air. *Your car is running well since I cleaned the carburettor.*

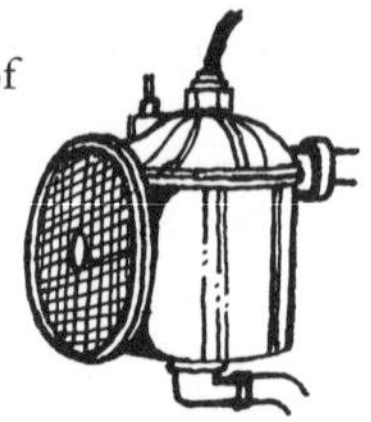

**driving-seat** /ˈdraiviŋsiːt/ seat for a car driver behind the *steering-wheel* (see below). *If you have long legs, move the driving-seat back.*

**engine** /ˈendʒin/ motor of a car etc. *The engine of a Volkswagen is at the back.*

**false** /fɔːls/ not true. *He is in prison because he used false number plates. False hair is very expensive.*

**file** /fail/ instrument that we can use to cut or mark steel. *The prisoner used a file to cut the window bars.*

**force** /fɔːs/ use strength to make something move. *The pump forces petrol up into the carburettor. The thieves forced their way into the garage.*

**job** /dʒɔb/ work; a piece of work. *Peter asked for a job at Robinson's garage. I want you to do a job on Lord Steel's car—check the carburettors.*

**number plate** /ˈnʌmbə pleit/ flat piece of steel with a number on it. *If you can't read a car number plate at twenty-five yards, you must not drive.*

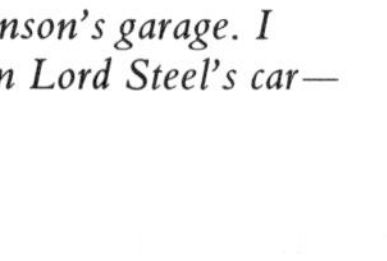


**petrol** /ˈpetrəl/ form of oil that drives car engines (in some English-speaking countries it is called *benzine* or *gasoline*). *Drive into the next petrol station and fill up. My car does about forty miles to the gallon (of petrol).*

**puncture** /ˈpʌŋktʃə/ hole which lets the air out of a tyre (see below). *Nails and other sharp things on the road can give you a puncture. They puncture your tyres.*

**run out** /ˈrʌn ˈaut/ come to the end (of something like petrol). *I can't write any more because I have run out of paper.*

**spare** /spɛə/ kept for use in the future. *If you are driving across Asia, you must carry a lot of spare parts. Take several spare tyres.*

**speedometer** /spiːˈdɔmitə/ instrument that shows the speed of a car. *Watch the speedometer and don't be caught speeding by the police.*

**steer** /stiə/ make a car (or ship) go to the right or left. *We use a steering-wheel to steer a car.*

**tank** /tæŋk/ place to store water etc. *The petrol tank is at the back of my car.*

**tool** /tuːl/ instrument that we can use to repair things. *The tools for this car are in a tool-box.*

**tyre** /ˈtaiə/ air-filled outer part of a wheel. *You need good tyres if you want to be safe on wet roads.*

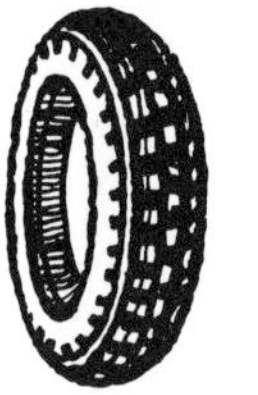

## "Tell him to blow"

PETER There's a chap on the telephone, sir. He says he has run out of petrol.

MANAGER How far away is he?

PETER He says he's at the corner of Bridge Street.

MANAGER That's less than half a mile away. Tell him to blow *hard* into the petrol tank.

PETER Did you say "blow" sir? . . . He doesn't understand.

MANAGER Then explain to him. Tell him that there'll still be a little petrol in the tank. If he blows really hard, he will force it up into the carburettor.

PETER (*to the manager, ten minutes later*) The gentleman has arrived, sir.

MANAGER Good! Well, fill him up then.

PETER I'm afraid it's a bigger job than that, sir.

MANAGER Why? What's happened?

PETER Well, sir, he blew into the petrol tank, but there was a sweet in his mouth—and——

MANAGER You mean——

PETER Yes, sir. He gave a good blow, and the sweet went into the tank.

---

## Exercise

**1** *Example* He must blow hard to force it into the carburettor.
*Answer* If he blows hard, he will force it into the carburettor.

1 He must look carefully to find the file.
2 You must turn this thing to empty the petrol tank.
3 They must watch the speedometer to know their speed.
4 He must finish the job to get his money.
5 You must mend the puncture quickly to receive a tip.
6 The mechanic must go to the store to get the spare parts.

**2** *Example* He *blew* very hard. (give-good)
*Answer* He gave a good blow.

1 They *walked* a long way. (go for-long)
2 She *slept* well. (have-good)
3 She *smiled* kindly. (give-kind)
4 The boy *shouted* loudly. (give-loud)
5 We *laughed* heartily. (have-good)
6 Have you *driven* far? (have-long)

## Car Thieves

One morning a Rolls Royce drove slowly into the garage where Peter was working. It had a flat tyre. Two men got out quickly. While they were in the manager's office, Peter looked at the car. He noticed that it had a German number plate. A few moments later the manager called him. "Find Jack," he said, "and help him to mend this puncture. Do it quickly because these gentlemen are going back to Germany tonight."

The men seemed to be worried about something. At last one of them said to his friend in German, "We'll go for a walk and come back in half an hour." Then the friend said the same thing to the manager in very bad English, and they both walked out of the garage.

Peter and Jack soon found out why the car had a puncture. There was a small file with a very sharp point in the tyre. Peter looked at the file with surprise.

"Strange!" he said. Then suddenly he ran to the car and opened the driving-seat door. "I thought so!" he cried. "The speedometer is marked in miles—and the steering-wheel is on the right. That number plate is false. Those men aren't German—their German is terrible—I think they're car thieves."

"Don't be stupid!" Jack said. "Car thieves wouldn't come to a garage just for a puncture."

"They had to!" Peter said. "Look. Their spare tyre is flat too!"

Peter and Jack went at once to see the manager. As soon as the manager had examined the car and the file, he telephoned the police. Two policemen arrived very quickly and hid in the garage.

The two men soon came back. "Well, is the car ready yet?" one of them asked. "We're in a great hurry."

At that moment the policemen came out of their hiding-places. "Can I see your passports, please, gentlemen?" one of them said.

The men's faces turned very white. "I don't understand," one of them answered.

"We don't speak English very well," said the other.

So the policeman introduced them to Peter. When Peter spoke to them in German they did not understand a word. "That's enough!" said the policeman at last. "We know who you are. This car belongs to Lord Steel and you took it from his garage in Patton Place. Right?"

"We're German visitors," one of the men said. But he had forgotten to speak in his "German accent".

"Really?" said the policeman. He showed them the little file. "Well, we think that you're English car thieves. But you made a bad mistake this time, didn't you? You used this file to open Lord Steel's garage door—and then you dropped the file in the road and ran over it. You must be more careful with your tools in future, *Herr* Smith!"

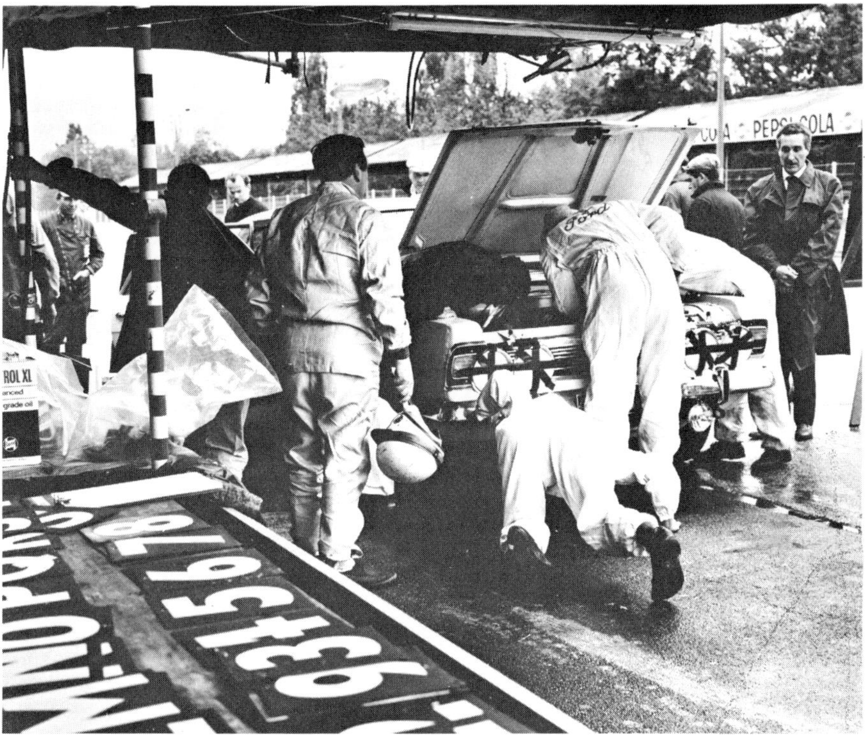


Car racing is popular but dangerous. The motor mechanic is the most important man in a racing driver's life. One mistake by the mechanic can cause many deaths. The ordinary mechanic's job is less exciting but he, too, must be careful.

# 1:5 A Hospital Nurse

**faint** /feint/ lose strength and feelings suddenly. *It was very hot, and several people fainted. Lie down if you feel faint.*

**groan** /grəun/ (give a) low cry of pain. *It was terrible to hear the patient's groans. She was in great pain all night and groaned again and again.*

**injection** /in'dʒekʃn/ use of a needle to put medicine through the skin into the body. *Doctors can give injections for many illnesses now. An injection doesn't hurt if the needle is sharp.*

**matron** /'meitrən/ head of all the sisters and nurses in a hospital. *The matron visits the wards every day; her eye never misses the smallest bit of dust.*

**patient** /'peiʃənt/ person who is ill. *The hospital has beds for 400 patients.*

**screen** /skri:n/ cloth on a frame to hide a bed in a hospital. "*The doctor wants to examine this patient. Please help me to put the screens round her bed.*" *The picture in a cinema or on TV comes on a screen.*

**serious** /'siəriəs/ (of illness) bad; dangerous. *He is in hospital with a serious illness. I'm afraid he's seriously ill.*

**sister** /'sistə/ head nurse in a ward. *A nurse needs special training and experience to become a sister. "Sister! Sister Brown! I'm feeling very sick."*

**student** /'stju:dənt/ person who is learning. *Anna is a student nurse. We talk about college students and school pupils.*

**surgeon** /'sə:dʒən/ doctor who cuts into a patient's body. *Mr Smith is a surgeon; don't call him Dr Smith. Heart surgeons did wonderful things in 1968.*

**thermometer** /θə'mɔmitə/ instrument that shows temperature. *Shake the thermometer carefully when you have read it.*

**training** /'treiniŋ/ preparing for work by giving or receiving lessons. *A girl can get training at King's College Hospital to become a nurse. The sisters there give young nurses a good training.*

**ward** /wɔ:d/ room with several beds in a hospital. *Visiting hours are the same in all the wards. My father is a patient in Pasteur Ward.*

## "That didn't hurt, did it?"

SISTER Anna, will you come to Ward No. 10 with me, please? There's an Italian patient who doesn't speak any English. Dr Roberts is with her, and he doesn't speak any Italian. Do you think you can help?

ANNA I hope I'll be able to understand Dr Roberts's English.

SISTER You'll be all right—This is Anna, Doctor, she's the Italian girl I told you about.

DOCTOR How do you do, Anna? I'm going to give this lady an injection in her arm. Will you please tell her that it won't hurt. I think she is afraid.
*Anna and the patient talk in Italian.*

ANNA She says she *is* afraid. But if the injection will save her life——

DOCTOR Tell her she needn't worry. Her illness is not at all serious. But if she wants to get completely well, she must have the injection.
*Anna and the patient talk in Italian.*

ANNA She wants the injection but she is afraid of the needle.

DOCTOR Talk to her, Anna. Say anything. Ask her where she lives—we'll give her the injection when she's not looking, sister. Have you got a second needle? We may need it.

SISTER Yes, doctor. Anna, don't stand too near the bed.

DOCTOR (*to patient*) There!—That didn't hurt, did it?—Where's Anna?

SISTER Poor girl! When she saw you put the needle in, she fainted.

---

## Exercise

**1** *Example* Where's the Italian patient? She doesn't speak any English.
*Answer* Where's the Italian patient who doesn't speak any English?

1 Where's the foreign lady? She needs an injection.
2 Where's the student nurse? She works in this ward.
3 Where's the surgeon? He wants to examine my wound.
4 Where's the sister? She always gives me my injections.
5 Where's the patient? He groans all night.
6 Where's the nurse? She uses this thermometer.

**2** *Example* I told you about an Italian girl. Her name is Anna.
*Answer* Anna's the Italian girl I told you about.

1 I was talking to a student nurse. Her name is Anna.
2 You were looking at a patient. His name is Jim.
3 I asked you about a surgeon. His name is Mr Black.
4 He introduced me to a hospital matron. Her name is Miss James.
5 They were looking for a sister. Her name is Mary Johnson.
6 I gave an injection to a patient. Her name is Mrs King.

## Men are big babies

Anna had always wanted to be a nurse. When she came to England, she applied for a job in a London hospital.

"I want to be a nurse, but I haven't had any training," she said to the matron.

"That doesn't matter. You'll start as a Student Nurse," answered the matron.

Anna earned very little money and the work was hard. But she enjoyed it. She made the beds, carried trays at meal times, and helped to wash patients. Sometimes she put the screens round the patients' beds during the surgeons' visits. She was able to watch the doctor and the nurses at work. She learnt a lot.

One morning Anna was alone in the men's ward. She was trying to push an empty bed. But she could not move it. Some of the men were drinking their tea. Others were reading. But when they saw Anna at work, they put down their cups and their books.

"You're too pretty to do hard work like that," said one young man. "Let me help you."

"You mustn't get out of bed, Mr MacGregor," Anna said.

"Call me Jim," said the young man. "I'm not ill any more. I'm leaving hospital tomorrow."

At that moment the man in the next bed began to groan.

"Oh, I've got a terrible pain."

Anna ran to the bed and looked at the man. He had only arrived that morning. He was young and good-looking. His face was rather white and his eyes were half shut.

"Hold my hand," he said to Anna. "I'm going to die."

Anna took his hand. "Where's the pain?" she asked anxiously.

"Everywhere," answered the young man. "All over my body."

"I'll call Sister," Anna said.

"No," said the young man. "Don't leave me."

"Jack's not really ill," said Jim. "He just wants to hold your hand. Why don't you take his temperature? Here's a thermometer."

Anna took the thermometer and put it in Jack's mouth. After two minutes she took it out and read it. Jack had a temperature of 108° Fahrenheit. "That's about 41° Centigrade!" Anna thought. She nearly died of fright. Jack quickly took the thermometer and read it himself.

"Help!" he cried. "I really *am* dying. Get a doctor at once!"

The Ward Sister heard the noise and came in. She soon found out about Jack's temperature. Jack did not have a temperature at all. Jim had put the thermometer in his tea.

The Sister smiled. "Men are big babies," she said to Anna. "Never listen to them. Next time you'd better call another nurse."

This baby doesn't like the injection but it will protect him.

Training for nurses is long and hard; but modern training methods are very good. New ideas are exchanged on International courses. The young nurses in the picture are on one of these courses in a British hospital.

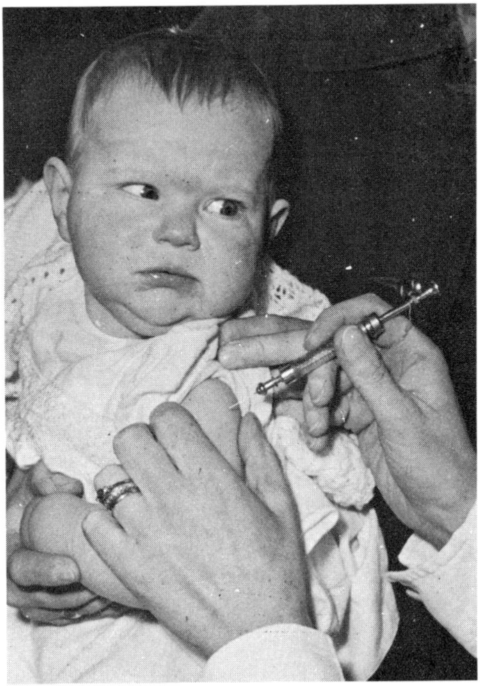

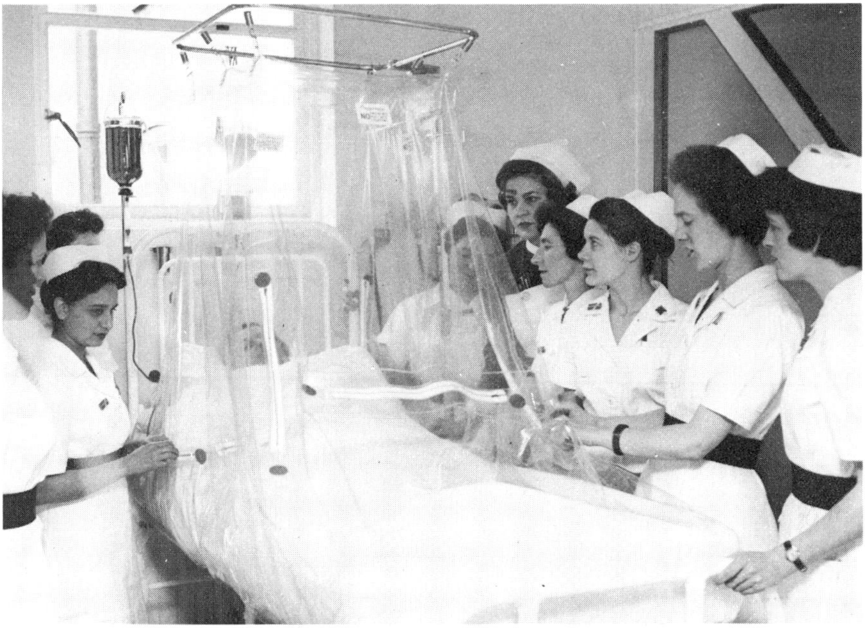

# 1:6 An Airport Reception Clerk

**book** /buk/ ask somebody to keep a place (a seat, a hotel room etc.) by writing one's name down. *Flight* AF83 *is fully booked* (= there are no more seats). *I want to book a single room for the night of 6 January.*

**Christian name** /ˈkristʃən neim/ first, or given, name. *His Christian names were Johann Sebastian and his surname was Bach.*

**counter** /ˈkauntə/ long table in an office or shop; a clerk or shop-assistant stands behind the counter to serve people. *You will find ear-rings at the jewellery counter over there, sir.*

**delay** /diˈlei/ being late; make something late. *Fog delays planes and trains. There was a delay of one hour on all flights.*

**departure** /diˈpɑːtʃə/ opposite of *arrival. We have an hour to wait between arrival at Orly airport at* 11.00 *and departure for Madrid at* 12.00.

**flight** /flait/ going through the air. *There are three flights a week from here to Buenos Aires. "Passengers for Flight* BE22 *to Berlin please go to the departure gate now."*

**fog** /fɔg/ cloud-like thickness of the air. *It is very dangerous to drive fast in fog. November is a foggy month in England.*

**hold on** /ˈhəuld ˈon/ wait. *Please hold on* (= do not put the telephone down).

**lounge** /laundʒ/ place (at an airport, in a hotel etc.) for people to sit. *Most hotels serve tea in the lounge.*

**runway** /ˈrʌnwei/ part of an airport like a wide road. *All three runways were busy; planes were landing or taking off every few minutes.*

**stick together** /ˈstik təˈgeðə/ be on the same side against outsiders. *We'll win if we stick together and stand shoulder to shoulder.*

**if you will excuse me** please allow me to go. *I have enjoyed our talk, but now, if you will excuse me, I must go and cook the dinner.*

**I'll see** I'll find out . . . *"My car's broken down."—"I'll see if I can make it go." "Are there any seats on the next plane?"— "I'll see."*

**until further notice** until we tell you something different. *Please send your letters to this address until further notice.*

## "If you don't mind——"

TOURIST I've just missed the BEA flight to Paris. Can you book me a seat on the next plane?

KARL I'll see if there's a seat on BE22, sir—No, I'm afraid the plane is completely full, and there isn't another flight until 18.00 hours.

TOURIST This is stupid. I left my hotel more than two hours ago in order to get here in time. And what happened? My taxi driver couldn't drive at more than 10 miles an hour because of the traffic.

KARL I'm sorry, sir. I'll try Air France for you. . . . No, I'm afraid all their planes are fully booked too.

TOURIST You English make me angry! Why can't you build better roads?

KARL I agree with you, sir. English traffic is very bad. Now, if you will excuse me, there's another gentleman here——

TOURIST It was the same yesterday. I flew from Manchester to London. I spent one hour at the airport, three-quarters of an hour in the plane —and three and a half hours on the road. When I reached my hotel in Piccadilly dinner was over!

KARL I'm sorry, sir. Now, if you don't mind——

TOURIST You English do everything slowly. Now in my country——

ENGLISHMAN So we're slow, are we? Then it's because of people like you. You talk too much!

KARL I really must attend to this gentleman, sir.

TOURIST You English always stick together!

KARL I'm not English, sir. I'm a foreigner—like you.

---

## Exercise

**1** *Example* I get very angry because of the English.
*Answer* The English make me very angry.

1 The traffic is slow because of fog.
2 He was late because of the traffic.
3 The passengers got angry because of the loudspeakers.
4 The runway was rather dangerous because of the snow.
5 All the flights were late because of the delay.
6 The patient became sleepy because of the injection.

**2** *Example* I wanted to get here in time, so I left two hours ago.
*Answer* I left two hours ago in order to get here in time.

1 He wanted to book a seat, so he went to the reception counter.
2 We wanted to find out our departure time, so we looked at the timetable.
3 I wanted to wait for the next plane, so I sat in the airport lounge.
4 Karl wanted to miss the traffic, so he left home very early.
5 He wanted to find out the time of his flight, so he listened to the loudspeaker.
6 The passenger wanted to ask a question, so he went up to the counter.

## The VIP

There was thick fog at Heathrow and snow on the runways. It was midday and the loudspeakers said again and again: "There will be no flights until further notice." But more and more people arrived at the airport. The restaurants, bars and lounges were all crowded. There were no empty seats in the great halls.

Karl had plenty to do. Passengers came up to the counter all the time. They asked questions about arrivals and departures, about luggage, about lost children. Suddenly a beautiful woman arrived at the counter. "I'm flying to Zurich," she said. "Here's my ticket."

"Yes, madam," said Karl, "but I'm afraid there's been a delay——"

"I know," the woman said. "That's why I'm here. I'm Mrs Max Stolberg." Karl knew all about Max Stolberg, the great film star. He was making a film in England at the moment. Karl had never seen Mrs Stolberg before, but he was not surprised that she was beautiful. "I'd be very happy to help you, madam," he said. "What can I do for you?"

Mrs Stolberg looked at Karl and smiled. "All the lounges and restaurants are full," she said. "It's very cold. Do you think that I could be a VIP?"

Karl smiled back. "The wife of Max Stolberg is a *Very* Important Person," he said. "Please sit here while I telephone the VIP room."

The man in the VIP room told him to look at Mrs Stolberg's passport. "A lot of people try that trick," he said. Karl did not like to ask Mrs Stolberg for her passport, but she smiled, took the passport out of her bag and opened it. There was her picture—and her name in large letters: "Mrs Linda Stolberg".

Karl took her upstairs to the VIP room. She thanked him and gave him a £1 tip. Then he went back to his counter. A few minutes later, the telephone rang.

"This is Max Stolberg. Any news of my wife yet?"

"Yes, sir," Karl answered. "She is waiting in the VIP room."

"Really?" Max Stolberg sounded surprised. "So there has been a flight from Zurich after all?"

"*From* Zurich, sir?" asked Karl. "Your wife says she's going *to* Zurich."

"Then she's not my wife," says Max Stolberg. "My wife telephoned five hours ago—from Zurich airport!"

"Hold on a minute, sir," Karl said. "I'll phone the man in the VIP room at once."

The man in the VIP room went away and came back after a few moments. "It's Mrs Max Stolberg, all right," he said.

When Karl told Max Stolberg this, he asked, "What was her Christian name?"

"Linda," said Karl.

Max Stolberg laughed. "Linda! Of course!" he cried. "She was my *first* wife. I've married several times, you know."

Airport receptionists are always busy. Because more people are travelling by air, they have to help passengers in many different ways: finding lost luggage or children, explaining delays and changing reservations. Their job is more difficult because London needs another airport. Although it already has London (Heathrow) and Gatwick Airport, it needs a third one.

# 1:7 An Exporter's Secretary

**abroad** /ə'brɔːd/ in (or to) another country. *More and more people go abroad for summer holidays. He lives abroad in order not to pay high taxes.*

**business** /'biznis/ work which needs an office; getting money by buying and selling etc. *Mr Pepper is a business man. He has a small business: about twenty people work for him.*

**the Continent** /'kɔntinənt/ Europe (all parts except the islands). *"Where's Tom?"—"He's somewhere on the Continent—perhaps in Italy." That restaurant is famous for its continental food.*

**desk** /desk/ writing-table in an office, school etc. *Does Mr Pepper really need such a big desk?*

**dictate** /dik'teit/ say words which another person then writes down. *Mr Pepper is dictating some letters to his secretary. She can take dictation at 150 words a minute.*

**export** (v.) /eks'pɔːt/ (n.) /'ekspɔːt/ sell goods (export them) to people in other countries; thing sold (export) to another country. *Britain exports large numbers of cars. The makers of these cars are exporters.*

**firm** /fəːm/ company, business company. *Mr Pepper's firm is a small one, but he does business with some very large continental firms.*

**import** (v.) /im'pɔːt/ (n.) /'impɔːt/ buy goods (import them) from other countries; goods (imports) that have come from other countries. *Britain imports most of her food. We are spending too much on imports.*

**message** /'mesidʒ/ words spoken by A to B, for B to say them to C. *If I am out, please leave a message with my secretary. Are there any telephone messages for me?*

**secretary** /'sekrətri/ person (usually a girl) who does office work for somebody. *"I'm afraid Mr Pepper is out. Will you speak to his secretary?"*

**tea-break** /'tiːbreik/ ten minutes when people stop work to drink tea.

**type** /taip/ use a machine (a *typewriter*) to write letters etc. *She is quite a good typist; she types at about sixty words a minute and makes no typing mistakes.*

**wholesale** /'həulseil/ buying and selling goods in large numbers. *Shopkeepers buy goods wholesale, from wholesalers; they sell them retail, singly or in small numbers.*

## "I know!"

YOUNG WOMAN Where is everybody? The office is empty.
ANNA It's the tea-break, madam. Can I help you?
YOUNG WOMAN Yes, I'd like to see Mr Pepper.
ANNA I'm afraid Mr Pepper is out, madam.
YOUNG WOMAN Really? He said he would be free at 4 o'clock.
ANNA I don't think he has returned yet. But please take a seat. I'll go to his office and see.
ANNA (*a minute later*) No, he's not there, madam. Would you like to wait or shall I take a message?
YOUNG WOMAN I'll wait.
ANNA I'm sure he won't be long, madam. Would you like to read the paper?
YOUNG WOMAN No, thank you. But I'd smoke a cigarette if I had one.
ANNA I'm sorry. I haven't got any. I don't smoke.
YOUNG WOMAN You're from abroad, aren't you? Do you like it here?
ANNA Do you mean England, or Pepper & Sons Ltd?
YOUNG WOMAN Well, both.
ANNA I like England very much, and I like the office too, but—— Are you a friend of Mr Pepper's?
YOUNG WOMAN Oh no!
ANNA Well, Mr Pepper's very kind, but he makes us work too hard. He doesn't understand that women aren't as strong as men.
YOUNG WOMAN You're quite right, my dear, I know! I'm his wife!

---

## Exercise

**1** *Example* Do you know if Mr Pepper has returned?
*Answer* I don't think Mr Pepper has returned yet.

1 Do you know if he has got my letter?
2 Do you know if he has ordered the shirts?
3 Do you know if he has had lunch?
4 Do you know if his wife has returned from Paris?
5 Do you know if she has received my telegram?
6 Do you know if they have found a new au pair girl?

**2** *Example* I'd smoke a cigarette. (have)
*Answer* I'd smoke a cigarette if I had one.

1 She'd take a message. (give her)
2 Mr Pepper would sell the shirts wholesale. (want)
3 My firm would export skirts. (order)
4 We'd enjoy some continental food. (cook)
5 She'd type your letters. (dictate)
6 Would you like a gold ring? (I buy)

## Six thousand skirts

Mr Pepper was very proud of his business. He was a very busy man. He sold clothes of all kinds to different countries. "Britain needs to export," he explained to Anna. "We must earn foreign money. Therefore, we must export more than we import." Anna did not really know much about business, but she spoke—and wrote—English very well. Her father had once spent two years in England and during that time she had gone to an English school. So Mr Pepper was able to dictate letters to her in English. And she was able to translate them into her own language.

One morning Mr Pepper called her into his office. He handed her a piece of paper. "Please translate this letter," he said. "I'm just going out. I won't be back until 4 o'clock. Leave the letter on my desk and I'll sign it then."

Anna took the letter back to the room where all the typists and secretaries worked. The letter was very short and it was very difficult to read. Mr Pepper's writing was terrible. She tried hard to understand it. She showed it to the other typists.

They studied the letter carefully together. The letter was addressed to a well-known continental wholesale firm. Mr Pepper's letter accepted their order for 6,000 grey skirts. It said that the skirts would be ready in a week. Anna soon translated the letter. Then she typed it and put it on Mr Pepper's desk.

Mr Pepper returned at 4.30. He rushed into his office, saw the letter and called again for Anna. "I don't understand your language," he said. "But I imagine it's all right."

"Well, sir," Anna began. "I'm not quite sure——"

But Mr Pepper was not listening. He signed the letter and gave it to Anna. "Post it at once. Don't forget to put a 4p stamp on it." Then he rushed out of the front door.

Three days later Mr Pepper came into the typists' room. He seemed very angry. "Anna!" he cried. "Please come into my office at once."

"What have I done wrong?" Anna wondered. She went into Mr Pepper's office and shut the door behind her. "You want to speak to me, sir?" she said.

"Yes, indeed I do!" Mr Pepper said. "Tell me—do your soldiers wear skirts?"

"Skirts?" Anna was surprised.

Mr Pepper looked at her and began to laugh. "6,000 skirts for the army! That really is a joke," he said. "I wrote *shirts*, not *skirts*, you stupid girl!"

The importer or exporter must have a really good office with good clerks and secretaries. He must also be able to book ships or aircraft. He does this through the Baltic Exchange which you see in the picture.

There are now more secretarial jobs than good secretaries. The head of the office—the "boss"—must offer good pay and a pleasant office to work in; a good secretary can choose a job which interests her. An exporter's secretary needs to be calm and helpful in this busy world.

The evening newspapers have many small notices (small-ads) about office jobs for men and women.

**SECRETARY** required for assistant managing director in large company in West London. Interesting and varied work in very pleasant private office. Five-day week, three weeks' annual holiday with this year's arrangements honoured. Apply to Box P84.

# 2

## FREE TIME AND HOLIDAYS

# 2:1 A Quiet Evening Out

**all right** /'ɔːl 'rait/ I agree. *"Let's go to the Starlight Coffee Bar."—"All right."*

**baby-sitting** /'beibisitiŋ/ spending the evening in another person's house to look after the children. *She earns some money by baby-sitting for parents who want to go out for the evening. It isn't easy to get a good baby-sitter.*

**bar** /bɑː/ high narrow table for drinks, or the room that it is in. *He's in the bar, having a pint of bitter. He's standing at the bar, talking to the landlord.*

**bitter** /'bitə/ kind of beer, a bitter drink. *A pint of bitter, please, landlord.*

**darts** /dɑːts/ little things with a point; game in which you throw these at a circle marked with numbers 1–20. *"Let's play darts. Where's the dart board?"*

**hero** /'hiərəu/ man who is most interesting to the reader of a story; the most interesting woman is the *heroine*. *The hero often marries the heroine, and the story ends: "And they lived happily ever after."*

**landlord** /'lænlɔːd/ manager of a pub. *Tom Brown is the landlord of the Three Feathers. You'll find the landlord in the public bar every evening.*

**lemonade** /'lemə'neid/ drink made from (or tasting like) a fruit juice. *She's very young; give her a glass of lemonade.*

**let's** /lets/ I think that it would be good to (do something). *Let's play some records. Let's hope that he will soon be better.*

**manager** /'mænidʒə/ head man in a hotel, shop, bank etc. *I am very angry and I want to see the hotel manager at once.*

**pub** (= public house) /pʌb/ house where anybody over the age of 18 can buy a drink. *My friends and I like to meet in the pub.*

**public** /'pʌblik/ (open to) everybody; all people (not only members). *The castle is open to the public. In a pub, you pay less for drinks in the public bar than in the other bars.*

**sport** /spɔːt/ games etc. *We often talk about sport—football, cricket, horse-racing etc.*

**"X" films** /'eks'filmz/ films that a cinema can show only to people more than 18 years old. *"AA" films can be shown only to people more than 14, and "A" and "U" films can be shown to anyone, although parents are advised that "A" films may contain scenes unsuitable for young children.*

## A date with John

ANNE Hello, John! How are you?
JOHN Fine. What about you? I phoned you twice this week, but got no answer.
ANNE I was baby-sitting; I've earned £1. Not bad, is it?
JOHN Clever girl! Are you free this evening? We could go out together.
ANNE I'd love to. Let's go to that new dance-hall in King's Road.
JOHN I'm afraid I can't dance. I hurt my leg in the game on Saturday.
ANNE Football! Stupid game! What about the cinema, then?
JOHN All right. Tom says there's a very good murder film at the Odeon. Let's have a drink first at the Black Horse. It's not far from the cinema.
ANNE Must we go to the pub?—Oh, all right! Where shall we meet?
JOHN At the Black Horse at 6 o'clock. And don't be late. It's going to be cold tonight.
ANNE I'm wearing my trouser suit, then—if you don't mind!
JOHN Yes, I do mind. I don't like girls in trousers.
ANNE Well, I don't like boys with long hair. If you had a hair-cut, I'd wear a skirt.
JOHN See you at six o'clock, then—in your trousers.

---

## Exercise

**1** *Example* Anne says she wants to wear her trouser suit this evening.
*Answer* I'm wearing my trouser suit—if you don't mind.

1 Anne says she wants to wear a long dress tomorrow night.
2 Anne says she wants to go to Paris next week.
3 Anne says she wants to have roast chicken tonight.
4 Anne says she wants to drink a glass of bitter next.
5 Anne says she wants to stay at home tonight.
6 Anne says she wants to wash her hair tomorrow.

**2** *Example* You won't have a hair-cut, so I won't wear a skirt.
*Answer* If you had a hair-cut, I would wear a skirt.

1 You won't play darts, so I won't take you to the pub.
2 I don't like the hero, so I won't see that film again.
3 They don't like sport, so we won't talk to them about it.
4 He doesn't drink bitter, so I won't buy him a pint.
5 You don't love me, so you won't marry me.
6 She doesn't like lemonade, so she won't accept a glass.

## "What'll you have?"

Anne and John met at the Black Horse at 6 o'clock.

"Let's go to a coffee-bar instead." said Anne.

"Why?" asked John.

"Because pubs are for men," answered Anne. "They're no fun for girls. You and your friends will just play darts together and talk about sport."

"Not tonight," said John. "Really I won't." He led her into the Public Bar. Anne sat down at a table near the door and John went to get the drinks. Suddenly somebody cried, "Hello, John!"

Anne looked up. It was Tom. Anne did not like him at all. He was very small and very ugly. He made stupid jokes.

"Come to the bar, Anne!" said Tom. "Don't sit there all alone." Anne got up slowly.

"What'll you have?" Tom went on. "A pint of bitter?"

"No, thank you," Anne began. "I'll have——"

"Oh, I forgot!" said Tom. "You don't drink, do you? You're not old enough. A glass of lemonade for the young lady, Landlord."

Anne's face was red. She said that she was nineteen, but the landlord did not believe her. He handed her a glass of lemonade and everybody laughed—even John. Anne was very angry. "You can stay here with your friends, if you like, John," she cried. "I'm going to the cinema."

"So am I," said Tom. "*Murder on a Mountain*—a very good film. See you later, then!"

"I hope not," said Anne. Then she walked straight out of the pub. John ran after her, put his arm round her and said he was sorry. At the cinema, John bought two tickets and they sat down. The cinema was almost empty.

At 8.30 the big picture began. At the same moment somebody whispered in Anne's ear, "This isn't a film for little girls. It's an 'X' film. I must tell the manager that you're too young!"

Anne turned round. It was Tom, of course. There were plenty of empty seats but he had sat down right behind them.

"Go away!" said John. "Why do you have to sit here and spoil things?"

"I can sit where I like, can't I?" said Tom. "It's a free country!"

Tom talked all the time. "Don't look!" he said each time the hero and the heroine were alone. "It's such a bad example for little girls!" John and Anne got up and changed their seats several times. But each time Tom changed his seat too.

At last Anne got really angry. She picked up her umbrella and hit Tom on the head.

"Ouch!" cried Tom. The manager arrived.

"What are you doing here?" he said to Tom. "You're making a lot of noise, *and* you're under 16. Didn't you see the notice? This is an 'X' film. Outside!"

Anne and John enjoyed the rest of the film in peace.

This is a cinema in Piccadilly Circus. A lot of people go to the cinema in London both in the afternoon and in the evening. Outside London, cinemas are almost empty except on Saturday evening.

English pubs have changed in the last ten years. Today a lot of young men take their wives or girl-friends to a pub for an evening out. Or they have a drink in one of the bars—the public bar or the saloon bar—before they go home. In towns, many people even have lunch in a pub. Some pubs have a room for a restaurant; other pubs sell snacks—sandwiches, hot sausages and pies. The car number plate over the bar means "Are you 18?" You cannot have strong drink if you are under 18 years old.

# 2:2 Week-end Shopping

**assistant** /əˈsistənt/ person who helps another; a shop-assistant sells goods in a shop. *We told the shop-assistant that we were looking for green stockings.*

**booth** /buːð/ small place with glass round it where one or two people can hear records. *A record shop usually has several booths.*

**boutique** /buːˈtiːk/ (French) shop—English name for a small shop of a special kind. *There are boutiques that sell only unusual clothes.*

**go with** /ˈgəu wið/ be all right with; look good with. *This shirt goes with my old brown suit but it doesn't go with my new blue one.*

**marvellous** /ˈmɑːvələs/ wonderful; very good. *We had a marvellous time in London.*

**nylon** /ˈnailən/ man-made thread and cloth. *Nylons* are stockings. *A nylon shirt dries very quickly.*

**pop music** /ˈpɔp ˈmjuːzik/ music and songs that most young people enjoy. *The BBC's "Radio 1" plays pop music and almost nothing else. You never hear pop songs on "Radio 3".*

**rail** /reil/ long bar of iron or wood etc. *The suits in that boutique hang from rails. A train runs on rails of another kind.*

**recording** /riˈkɔːdiŋ/ record that one person or group has made. *There are very many recordings of Mendelssohn's "Song without Words" No. 30 in A.*

**silk** /silk/ thread from a small animal; material made from silk thread. *Before there were nylons, women wore silk stockings. I carry a silk handkerchief in my pocket.*

**size** /saiz/ how big something is. *John takes size 9 in shoes. This shirt isn't my size.*

**style** /stail/ the way somebody makes or does something. *"I don't like the style of that shirt. The high neck is stupid." Every good writer has his own style.*

**try on** /ˈtrai ˈɔn/ put (clothes) on, and in this way find out if they look and feel right. *Older women love to try on hats. I want to try the coat on.*

**turn down** /ˈtəːn ˈdaun/ turn something to make the lights less bright or the sound less loud etc. *Of course you may play records, but turn the sound down because the baby is asleep.*

**What about . . . ?** /ˈwɔt əbaut/ *What about this shirt?* = Look at this shirt, Do you like it?
*What about me?* = Don't forget me.

## Pop Records

JOHN (*to shop-assistant*) We want to hear the Baby Elephants' latest recording.

ANNE That group? No, thank you! They make too much noise. I hate noisy music. I want to hear "Love Me in the Clouds".

ASSISTANT Which recording? Frankie Mott's or Prunella Prune's?

ANNE Oh, Frankie Mott's, of course.

JOHN Frankie Mott? He's terrible. Even old George can sing better.

ANNE Well, I like him.

ASSISTANT Number 3 booth is free. I'll put the record on for you.

ANNE Could you also put on Frankie's "Girl in a Trouser Suit"? I heard him singing it on Radio 1 yesterday.

JOHN So did I, and I don't want to hear it again. "I love my girl in a trouser suit"! Really! It's stupid.

ANNE You don't have to listen to it. You can wait, or go into another booth.

JOHN All the other booths are full.

ASSISTANT There'll be one free in a minute.

JOHN No. I'll go in with her. Put the record on, please—It's too loud.

ANNE Turn it down, then.—No, that's not loud enough. You can hear the record in the next booth. It sounds like Wagner.

JOHN That's not Wagner. That's *The Ride of the Long-Haired Boys*, by the Baby Elephants.

---

## Exercise

**1** *Example* He sang it on Radio 1. I heard him.
*Answer* I heard him singing it on Radio 1.

1 He hung the nylon shirts on a rail. I saw him.
2 The assistant turned down the lights. We watched her.
3 You tried on that marvellous dress. Your friend saw you.
4 Mary Jones sang the latest pop song. We heard her.
5 He played the latest recording of "Remember". They all heard him.
6 A lot of girls were buying men's shirts in the boutique. John saw them.

**2** *Example* I think it's Wagner—by the sound of it.
*Answer* It sounds like Wagner.

1 I think it's silk—by the feel of it.
2 I think it's coffee—by the smell of it.
3 I think it's butter—by the taste of it.
4 I think it's the Beatles—by the sound of it.
5 I think it's nylon—by the feel of it.
6 I think it's medicine—by the look of it.

## Carnaby Street

Anne did not like John's shirts. She said that the style was wrong and that the colours were too bright.

"I'll buy you one!" she cried. "I'd like to give you a present."

So the next morning they took a bus to Piccadilly Circus and walked to Carnaby Street.

They walked into three shops, looked at the shirts, and walked out again. "The colours are terrible," Anne explained. "They aren't right for you." At last she stopped in front of a very modern boutique. "This is the one!" she cried. John looked inside. It was very dark, and a record-player was playing pop music.

A good-looking shop-assistant in narrow trousers and a bright yellow shirt came forward. "Can I help you?" he said to Anne.

Anne smiled. "Can you show me some shirts—some really modern ones?"

"Of course," said the assistant. "What size?"

"Size 16," John answered.

The assistant took them to a rail where hundreds of shirts were hanging—cotton shirts, nylon shirts, silk shirts with high necks. John soon saw one that he liked. But Anne said that the colour did not suit his eyes.

"All right, then," said John, "I'll have this one." But Anne said that it was not modern enough.

"What about this one?" said the assistant. It was a blue shirt with white flowers on it.

"I don't think it would really suit you, John," said Anne. "But it would suit me. Don't you think so? I need a new shirt for my trouser suit."

John opened his mouth. He wanted to say that he did not like the shirt and that he hated Anne's trouser suit. But the assistant answered first. "It's one of our loveliest shirts," he said. "All the girls love it. In fact we sell more to girls than to boys."

John suddenly noticed that the shop was full of girls. They were all buying men's clothes. "Can I try on the shirt in a smaller size?" asked Anne.

"Of course," said the assistant.

Two minutes later, Anne came out from behind a curtain. She was wearing the shirt. "It's marvellous!" she cried. "I'll take it—Oh, John! Your present!"

"Don't worry," said John. "Let's go to a girls' boutique. I'm sure we'll find something there!"

"Good idea!" said Anne. "I saw a marvellous trouser suit in the shop round the corner. I need a new one to go with my new shirt."

You can still shop cheaply in London's markets. Do you want buttons from the time of Queen Victoria for your new coat? Do you want meat for your Sunday lunch? You will find them in one of the Saturday markets. The older markets sell food, shoes and clothes. But there are now many new markets which sell almost anything.

# 2:3 Amateur Mechanics

**brakes** /breiks/ parts which stop a car, bicycle etc. *The brakes on a bicycle slow down or stop the wheels.*

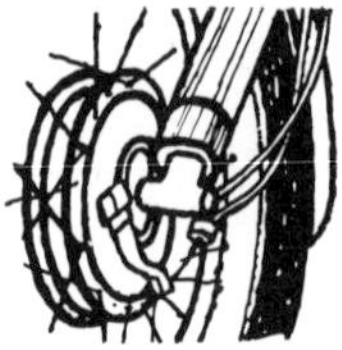

**carburettor** /'kɑ:bjuretə/ part of a petrol engine; it mixes petrol and air. *John's motor-bike is running well since he cleaned the carburettor.*

**engine** /'endʒin/ machine to drive a car, motor-bike, pump etc. *The engine of a Volkswagen is at the back.*

**magneto** /mæg'ni:təu/—The petrol and air mixture from the carburettor goes into the engine; an electric spark (sudden fire) fires it there; in some engines a *magneto* makes this spark.

**match** /mætʃ/ small stick with something at one end to make fire. *Have you got a box of matches in your pocket?*

**motor-bike** /'məutəbaik/ (also *motor-cycle*) bicycle with a petrol engine. *You drive a car but you ride a motor-bike.*

**nut** /nʌt/—You put a *nut* on the end of a *bolt* and turn it round and round; the bolt and nut lock two pieces of iron etc. together. *You turn a nut with a spanner.*

**oil-can** /'ɔilkæn/ small can or tin of oil with a long neck. *I use this oil-can for my sewing-machine.*

**petrol** /'petrəl/—*Petrol* ("benzine" in some countries) looks like water but it burns easily in car engines etc. *You get petrol at a filling station.*

**pillion** /'piljən/ seat for one person behind the seat for the rider of a motor-bike. *Young men often carry their girl-friends on their pillions.*

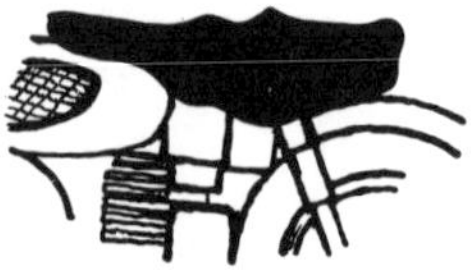

**properly** /'prɔpəli/ in the right way. *If you clean something properly, it will shine.*

**shed** /ʃed/ hut for garden things, bicycles etc. *We keep the garden chairs in the shed.*

**spanner** /'spænə/ instrument to turn a nut or bolt. *Use an ordinary spanner on this nut.*

**tank** /tæŋk/ part of a car etc. that carries petrol. *Fill the tank with petrol.*

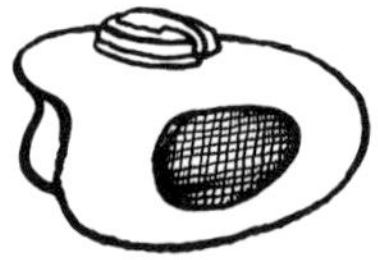

**tool** /tu:l/ instrument that we use to repair a machine etc. *Hammers, axes and spanners are tools.*

**wire** /'waiə/ length of iron etc. like hard string. *We use wire for fences etc.*

**wreck** /rek/ destroy. *"Drive carefully. Don't wreck my car."*

**just in time** /'dʒʌst in 'taim/ only a moment before something else. *He arrived at 5.59, just in time to catch the 6.00 bus.*

A **mechanic** /mi'kænik/ works on machines. An **amateur mechanic** /'æmətə: mi'kænik/ works on machines because he enjoys the work—not for pay.

## "Do you want any help?"

MOTHER What's that thing on the table?
JOHN It's the carburettor from my motor-bike, Mum.
MOTHER There's an oil mark on the clean table-cloth! Look! And there's another on the floor. Take the thing outside. You've got a shed.
JOHN It's cold in the shed.
MOTHER Well, I want to lay the table.
FATHER Who has been taking things from my tool-bag?—Oh, it's you, is it? Who said you could borrow my spanner?
JOHN I lent you my spanner after you had lost yours!
FATHER Well, all right. But next time you'd better ask.—Do you want any help?
JOHN No, thank you, Dad.
FATHER You haven't fixed that nut properly. Here! Give me the spanner.
JOHN Dad, I don't need your help, really. I'm——
FATHER If you leave it like that, it'll fall off.
JOHN Dad, I'm trying to explain to you——
FATHER (*takes spanner*) You boys think you know everything. I had a motor-bike before you were born.
JOHN I know, Dad. You've told me that before—What are you doing?
FATHER I'm fixing this nut. It's dangerous like this. Just a little strength, that's all you need!
JOHN Quite right, Dad. But I was taking the nut *off*! Now I can't move it at all.

---

## Exercise

**1** *Example* You can borrow my spanner.
*Answer* Who said you could borrow my spanner?

1 They can stop for tea.
2 He will lock the shed.
3 You want better brakes on your car.
4 A mechanic will be able to mend it.
5 You can take your girl-friend on the pillion.
6 We repair engines with spanners.

**2** *Example* You lost your spanner. Then I lent you mine.
*Answer* I lent you my spanner after you had lost yours.

1 You gave me your box of matches. Then I found mine.
2 She had an accident with her car. Then she wrecked mine.
3 He cleaned our carburettor. Then he cleaned hers.
4 I filled my petrol tank. Then you filled yours.
5 He built his shed. Then he helped me to build mine.
6 You fixed your magneto. Then you mended hers.

## The motor-bike

One Saturday evening, Anne rang the bell at John's house. John's mother opened the door. "I think John is still in his shed," she said.

"What is he doing?" asked Anne.

"Repairing his motor-bike," his mother answered. "I'd like to throw that motor-bike away. He'll have an accident one day."

Anne went into the shed. There was a strong smell of oil. John was sitting beside his bike. He had a spanner in one hand and an oil-can in the other. He was very proud of his bike. It was an old machine, but he had built a new engine for it. "Hello!" he said, when he saw Anne. "I've almost finished. Give me the carburettor—No, stupid! That's a magneto!"

Anne watched John while he was fixing the carburettor. "You are clever!" she said.

"Oh, it's easy when you know how," said John. He mended a broken wire and put a new lamp in the tail light. Then he tried the brakes. "Fine!" he said. "Now she's ready for the road." He cleaned his hands, opened the shed door, and pushed the motor-bike into the street. "Would you like a ride?" he asked Anne.

Anne did not enjoy rides on John's motor-bike. He went very fast, and she was always frightened. Anne climbed unhappily on to the pillion.

"I've forgotten the petrol," John suddenly said. "I'll get a can from the garage while you take the top off the tank."

Anne got off the bike. She did not know where the tank was, and it was dark. She remembered that there was a box of matches in her bag. By the light of a match she soon found the tank. She took off the top and looked in. "John!" she shouted. "Don't worry. The tank is nearly full."

At that moment the match burnt her fingers. "Ouch!" she cried, and dropped the match. It fell right into the petrol tank. Anne jumped back just in time. The next moment pieces of the motor-bike were flying through the air. John's parents rushed out of the house.

"Are you hurt?" John's father asked.

Anne was crying. "I don't think so," she said. "But look at the motor-bike! I've completely wrecked it."

"Wonderful!" John's mother said in Anne's ear. "You were clever, my dear!"

John, of course, did not agree.

If all motor-cyclists wore helmets to protect their heads, fewer would be killed. Young people love speed and many buy motor-bikes as soon as they are old enough. Motor-bike scrambling is an exciting way of spending a week-end. In a scramble, the cyclists race across country, up hills and through woods and fields.

# 2:4 Dancing

**band** /bænd/ group of people who play music. *There was quite a big band but only the drums and one trumpet were good.*

**chap** /tʃæp/ man, fellow. *John's a nice chap. Most of the other chaps like him.*

**couple** /ˈkʌpl/ two people; a man and a woman. *There were only a few couples on the dance floor. Mr and Mrs Smith are a nice couple.*

**drum** /drʌm/ instrument of music that you beat (hit) with sticks. *There was a roll of drums and then the band played "God Save the Queen".*

**foxtrot** /ˈfɔkstrɔt/ modern dance. *The foxtrot came to Europe from America.*

**jacket** /ˈdʒækit/ short coat. *In a suit the jacket and trousers are of the same material.*

**leap year** /ˈliːp jəː/ 1968, 1972, 1976 etc. *In a leap year February has 29 days and the girl asks the man to marry her (instead of the man asking the girl).*

**mind** /maind/ be careful (of). *Mind my feet* = Don't step on my feet.

**promise** /ˈprɔmis/ say that one *will* do something (not "perhaps"). *"He promised to be here at 6; it is 6 now, and he has just arrived. He always keeps his promise. If he makes a promise, he doesn't break it."*

**quickstep** /ˈkwikstep/ modern dance, a fast foxtrot. *Beginners don't like the quickstep because it is so quick.*

**start** /stɑːt/ begin *The dance starts at 9.30; let's be there for the start. When are you going to start working?*

**tight** /tait/ in a way that makes it hard to move; holding with strength. *This is a very tight nut; I need a big spanner. "The bus is starting. Hold tight."*

**trumpet** /ˈtrʌmpit/ wind instrument of music. *Bill plays the trumpet in the school band.*

**turn on, turn off** /ˈtəːn ˈɔn (ˈɔf)/—You *turn on* an electric light, and it shines; you *turn off* the light, and darkness returns.

**waltz** /wɔːls/ dance. *John likes the modern slow waltz. Anne waltzes very well.*

## "Mind my feet!"

BOY Nice waltz, this.
GIRL It isn't a waltz. It's a quickstep.—Mind my feet!
BOY Sorry! I'm not a good dancer.
GIRL Don't worry about that.—You're holding me too tight.—That's better! Haven't you ever had any dancing lessons?
BOY No, never. Will you teach me?
GIRL I can't teach you here. There are too many people on the dance-floor.
BOY I didn't mean here. I meant at home.
GIRL Is your living-room big enough?
BOY Yes, and I've got a lot of good records. Do you like——?
GIRL Be careful! Why did you turn that way?
BOY I had to go that way because of that other couple.
GIRL Ouch! You've stepped on my foot again. You're talking too much. You're not listening to the music.
BOY It isn't a very good band, is it?
GIRL Yes, I think it's a very good band indeed.
BOY I think the leader is terrible. He can't play that trumpet——
GIRL He's my brother.
BOY Oh dear! I don't think you'll want to teach me now, will you?
GIRL I won't be able to.
BOY Why not?
GIRL Because I won't be able to stand up tomorrow. You've wrecked my feet!

---

## Exercise

**1** *Example* Do you want to teach me to dance?
*Answer* I don't think you want to teach me to dance.

1 Does she want to help you to walk? (I don't think—)
2 Do they want to teach us to waltz?
3 Does he want to train them to sing?
4 Do you want to learn to play the trumpet?
5 Does she want to start to learn the foxtrot?
6 Do you want to promise to be here early?

**2** *Example* You've never had any dancing lessons.
*Answer* Haven't you ever had any dancing lessons?

1 He's never heard a good dance band.
2 They've never played the trumpet.
3 He's never been to a school dance.
4 You've never learnt to waltz.
5 She's never broken a promise before.
6 You've never seen a couple dance the quickstep like that.

## A dance at the old school

John wanted to take Anne to a dance in the big new hall of his old school.

"Wear that short skirt you bought the other day," John said.

"No," said Anne. "I don't like short skirts for dances. I'm going to wear my long dress."

"All right," said John. "I was going to wear my new jacket and the pink shirt you bought me. Now I'll wear my suit instead."

When they reached the hall, most of the girls were wearing short dresses. Only four boys were wearing suits. "I told you so," John said rather angrily.

The dance had already started. Some of the teachers were there, with their wives. A group of boys had formed a band. They played rather badly, but they made a lot of noise. John and Anne danced two dances together. Then there was an "Excuse me" waltz.

"I hate these dances," John said. "Let's sit this one out."

"No," said Anne. "I like 'Excuse me' dances. You meet interesting people." They started to dance. At once a boy touched John on the shoulder. "Excuse me," he said. It was George.

"Oh, go away, George," said John.

"No, I won't!" said George. "Another chap has taken Mary away from *me*. So I'm going to take Anne away from *you*."

"Sorry, John," said Anne. "I can't say no, can I? We'll have the next dance together."

"All right." John went away and looked for Mary. She was dancing with a very short man. "Excuse me," said John, and took Mary away. He enjoyed his dance with her, but he did not ask her again. Mary was a better dancer than Anne, but John liked Anne better.

The next dance was a "Leap Year" quickstep. In "Leap Year" dances the girls ask the boys, not the boys the girls. The band started to play. At the same time somebody turned off most of the lights. John looked for Anne, but he could not find her anywhere. "She's dancing with somebody else," he thought bitterly. She had already spoken about "Leap Year" dances. "I won't ask you," she had warned him, "I'll ask somebody else—somebody I don't know. Girls don't often get that chance."

Suddenly he saw her. She was dancing with another man, and she was smiling and talking brightly. John could not see very well, but he was sure it was George.

John was very angry indeed. He rushed forward, took the man's arm and pulled him away from Anne. "She promised *me* this dance, you——" Then he stopped. He had made a mistake. It was not George. It was the headmaster.

What a difference! A London discotheque and competition ballroom dancing. Young people like the freedom of modern dancing and listening to the latest pop records. But ballroom dancing is still popular and competitions are shown every week on television.

# 2:5 Parties

**biscuit** /ˈbiskit/ rather hard, flat little cake. *She eats a lot of biscuits between meals.*

**carpet** /ˈkɑːpit/ large piece of soft material for the floor (*soft* is the opposite of hard). *A wall-to-wall carpet is expensive, but it is very nice in a bedroom or sitting-room.*

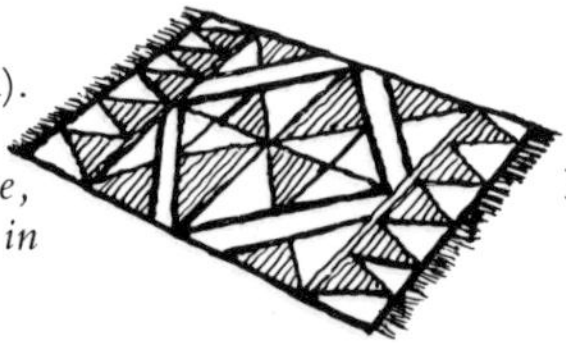

**cider** /ˈsaidə/ drink made from apples. *Some of the best cider in the world comes from the west of England.*

**gate-crasher** /ˈgeitkræʃə/ person who comes to a party but who was not invited. *A big man is useful at a party; he can throw the gate-crashers out.*

**landing** /ˈlændiŋ/ place at the top of the stairs outside the bedroom and bathroom doors. *Jane is using the telephone on the landing.*

**sausage** /ˈsɔsidʒ/ meat cut very small and pushed into a pipe-like skin. *Fried eggs and sausages make a very good breakfast.*

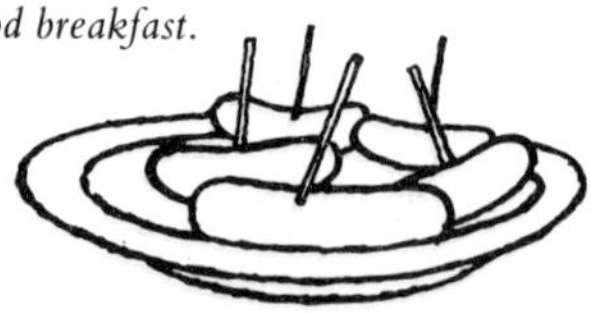

**stain** /stein/ mark that we can't wash out of something. *Ink makes bad stains on table-cloths. Fruit will also stain the cloth.*

**stranger** /ˈstreindʒə/ person we have not met before. *"I don't know that man. He's a stranger."*

**suppose** /səˈpəuz/ believe something to be true. *I suppose (that) you want to learn English. You like parties, I suppose.*

**teenage** /ˈtiːneidʒ/ between thirteen and nineteen years old. *A teenage party is sometimes noisy. Teenagers are people but some older people forget that.*

**Help yourself** /ˈhelp jɔːˈself/ Take the things that you want; do not wait until somebody passes them to you. *Help yourself to a hot sausage.*

**I don't think we've met** really means "I *know* that you and I have not been introduced."

## Talking to Strangers

JOHN Would you like a cigarette?
GIRL I don't smoke, thank you.
JOHN I don't smoke cigarettes either. I smoke a pipe.
GIRL I don't like the smell of a pipe.
JOHN Oh! Will you have a drink, then? I'll get you a glass——
GIRL I don't drink, thank you.
JOHN But you eat, I suppose! These biscuits are good. Have one.
GIRL No, thank you. I don't eat sweet things. They make me fat.
JOHN It's hot in here. Would you like to go into the garden?
GIRL What for? You can't see the flowers in the dark.
JOHN That's true! What would you like to do, then?
GIRL I don't know.
JOHN (*after a moment*) Well, let's just sit and talk, then. Have you been to many parties this year?
GIRL No, I don't like parties very much.
JOHN Really? Why not?
GIRL There's nothing to talk about.
JOHN Excuse me. Anne is calling me. (*to Anne*) Who is that terrible girl?
ANNE Rosemary James? Didn't you know? She's that marvellous tennis player. She taught me how to play.
JOHN That explains it. I hate girls who are good at games!
ANNE Really? (*She smiles*) You must hate *me* then; you never win when you play against me.

---

## Exercise

**1** *Example* make—sweet things—fat—me—always
*Answer* Sweet things always make me fat.

1 her—made—bad food—ill—never
2 plenty of exercise—thin—usually—people—keeps
3 never—made—cider—less thirsty—him
4 kept—usually—the baby—a biscuit—quiet
5 the carpets—wet shoes—often—dirty—make
6 me—always—makes—cutting sandwiches—tired

**2** *Example* I can play tennis. She taught me.
*Answer* She taught me how to play tennis.

1 I can make sandwiches. She showed me.
2 We can cook sausages. You taught us.
3 He can drink cider. A stranger showed him.
4 You can ride a motor-bike. Your teenage friend taught you.
5 They can repair the sofa. The assistant showed them.
6 I can't draw horses. Nobody taught me.

## Gate-crashers

One morning Anne phoned John. "My parents are going out this evening," she told him. "They say we can have a party. How many people shall we ask?"

"Not more than twenty," John said. "Your house is not very big."

During the afternoon Anne prepared the food. She cut sandwiches and cooked a large number of small sausages. At 8 o'clock the guests began to arrive, each with one or two bottles. At 9 o'clock the house was full. There were about forty or fifty people, but Anne didn't know them all. George put on the records and some couples tried to dance. They danced in the hall, on the landing, even in the bathroom. Everybody seemed very happy.

"Marvellous party!" said a fat boy with a red face.

"Glad you like it!" Anne said. "Have a sausage."

"I'd rather have another drink," the boy answered.

"Help yourself," Anne said. "There's some cider on the table over there."

Suddenly there was a crash. The fat boy had sat on the table and broken it. There were pieces of glass all over the floor and a large brown stain on the blue carpet.

"Sorry!" said the fat boy. "It was an accident." Anne looked for John. "Why did you invite that terrible boy?" she asked angrily.

"I didn't ask him," said John. "I thought he was one of *your* boy-friends."

At that moment there was a cry: "Something's burning!" Smoke was coming from the sofa. Somebody had dropped a cigarette on it.

"Oh!" Anne cried. "Our new sofa! Mother will kill me! What can we do?"

"We'll throw them all out!" John said. "They're not our friends. They're gate-crashers. Come on, George!"

Throwing out the gate-crashers was not easy. Some of them had drunk too much. But after five minutes John and George pushed the last of them into the street. When John came back into the living-room, he suddenly stopped. Anne was sitting on the sofa with a dark-haired boy. The boy's arm was round her. John went to the sofa. "I don't think we've met," he said to the boy. "Will you introduce us, Anne?"

Anne's face was red. "This is—er—. He—er—"

"Call me Pete," the boy said. Then he turned to John. "Get me a drink, will you? I'm thirsty."

John got Pete a drink. He picked up a full bottle of cider and poured it down his neck. "Sorry!" he said. "It was an accident. But you're all wet. You'll have to go home now, won't you?"

A cheese party does not cost very much, and most parties for young people are like this. At a "bring a bottle" party each guest brings a bottle of wine or beer. The host buys the food and provides the glasses.

In Scotland there are two big parties every year. Hogmanay—Scottish New Year—is an all-night party. Robert Burns' birthday on the 25th January is celebrated by Scots throughout the world.

# 2:6 Watching Football

**bottom** /ˈbɔtəm/ lowest part. *There are rocks at the bottom of the sea.*

**crowd** /kraud/ great number of people. *Listen to the noise of the crowd. Thousands of people crowded into the street.*

**division** /diˈviʒn/—The best football teams are in the First Division. A team at the bottom of the First Division will perhaps go down to Second Division.

**fan** /fæn/ person who finds everything about a team or a film star etc. interesting. *Football fans sometimes get too excited and break things.*

**foul** /faul/ play which is not allowed (off-side, hands, pushing another player etc.). *For a bad foul the player is sent off* (= off the field).

**goal** /gəul/ uprights and cross-bar of wood; place at which football players aim; the *goalkeeper* tries to "save" = to keep the ball out of the goal.

**home** /həum/—You play a *home* match on your own field; a game on the other team's field is an *away* match for you. *We'll win when we play them at home* = on our ground.

**match** /mætʃ/ game between two sides. *We're playing a match against the Police College next Saturday.*

**penalty** /ˈpenəlti/ special free-kick for a foul by a player near his own goal. *Only the goalkeeper can try to save the goal from a penalty kick.*

**referee** /refəˈriː/ man who watches the players and makes them play properly; *ref* is a short form. *He is a good referee; he knows the laws of the game.*

**rough** /rʌf/ dangerous; fighting instead of playing cleverly. *They're a rough team; they turn a friendly match into a battle.*

**score** /skɔː/ kick the ball into the goal; win points in a game. *Chelsea scored* (*a goal*) *in the last minute.*

**shot** /ʃɔt/ kick that is aimed at the goal. *What a shot!* = That was a very good shot OR That was a very bad shot.

**support** /səˈpɔːt/ help; give strength to; the *supporters* of a football team shout and sing to help their side.

**team** /tiːm/ eleven men playing football together, fifteen men playing Rugby football etc. *Have they picked the team for the match against Oxford?*

**tough** /tʌf/ hard, with great strength. *Good soldiers are tough.*

**whistle** /ˈwisl/ small instrument that you blow to make people pay attention.

## "Come on, Coventry!"

COVENTRY SUPPORTER My little brother could play better! Look at that chap in the middle of the field. Why's he rolling about on the ground?

CHELSEA SUPPORTER He was pushed from behind.

COVENTRY SUPPORTER He wasn't pushed! He just fell down.

CHELSEA SUPPORTER I've never seen such a bad foul! Send him off, ref.

COVENTRY SUPPORTER Why all the noise? You've got a free-kick, haven't you?

CHELSEA SUPPORTER Penalty, ref! That's better! He has given us a penalty—GOAL!

COVENTRY SUPPORTER Send off the ref—Coventry! C-O-V-E-N-T-R-Y!

CHELSEA SUPPORTER Be quiet! And move your head. I can't see.

COVENTRY SUPPORTER Then take your big feet off my new shoes! . . . Here! I've got a question for you. Why is Chelsea so near the bottom of the First Division?

CHELSEA SUPPORTER We won our last match.

COVENTRY SUPPORTER Come on, Coventry! You can do better than that!

CHELSEA SUPPORTER We won our last match—or didn't you know?

COVENTRY SUPPORTER No, I didn't. I was on holiday. I've come straight from the airport. Who were you playing against? Was it a girls' school?

CHELSEA SUPPORTER Shoot! What a shot! Come on, Chelsea! No, it wasn't a girls' school, but they played like girls.

COVENTRY SUPPORTER Wait till you play against *us* at home!

CHELSEA SUPPORTER We've already done that. That was the match that I was telling you about. We won, 4–1.

---

## Exercise

**1** *Example* Somebody pushed him from behind.
*Answer* He was pushed from behind.

1 Somebody blew a whistle.
2 Players scored three goals in the first half.
3 The players played the match in the rain.
4 Somebody took the excited fans to the police station.
5 The referee sent two players off for rough play.
6 Something hurt the goalkeeper very badly.

**2** *Example* That was a very bad foul. (I—see)

*Answer* I've never seen such a bad foul.

1 This is a very big crowd. (I—see)
2 He's a very tough player. (They—see)
3 It was a very fine shot. (The fans—see)
4 He was a very good referee. (Nobody—see)
5 They are very noisy supporters. (Nobody—hear)
6 He's a very bad dancer. (Anne—meet)

## A win for Chelsea

John was a Chelsea supporter. He had bought two tickets for the match with Liverpool, and had decided to ask Anne. They reached the ground early, and found a place behind the goal. Anne did not know anything about football.

"Why did the referee blow his whistle then?" she asked.

"He has just given a free-kick because a Liverpool player was off-side."

"What's 'off-side'?"

"I can't explain that. You wouldn't understand."

"He has blown his whistle again. Why?"

"Because a Liverpool player kicked a Chelsea player. That's a foul."

Suddenly a boy pushed in front of Anne. "Well! well!" he shouted in her ear. "It's our little girl. I didn't know she liked football!" It was Tom. He was wearing a paper hat with "LIVERPOOL" on the front of it.

"Why are you wearing that hat?" John cried angrily. "You don't support Liverpool."

"I know," said Tom. "But I don't like Chelsea. They're too rough. If they win this match, they'll meet Arsenal next, and I'm an Arsenal fan."

"Chelsea aren't rough. They're tough!" cried John, "and they're cleverer than Arsenal."

At half-time there was no score. John said that he had counted only seven shots at goal—all by Chelsea. Tom said that he had counted twenty-five fouls—all by Chelsea.

"Well," said John, "the referee only gave six free-kicks, and four of them were against Liverpool."

Anne said that she had not seen any shots or fouls. She had only seen the back of Tom's head.

The second half was harder than the first, and the crowd began to get very excited. Suddenly a Liverpool player took the ball. He ran past one Chelsea player, then past another. Soon there was only the goalkeeper in front of him. The Chelsea goalkeeper rushed out of his goal, and at the same time the Liverpool player kicked. He aimed at the far corner of the goal. It was a great shot. It flew hard and high.

"Goal!" shouted Tom.

"No! He missed!" shouted John.

The ball just touched the top of the cross-bar. It flew into the crowd behind the goal—and hit Tom right on the nose.

"That hurt!" cried Tom. "Dirty play!"

Two minutes later, Chelsea scored. Then the referee blew his whistle. Chelsea had won.

"Did you enjoy the game?" John asked Anne.

"Yes," said Anne. "I only saw the ball once, but that was a splendid shot."

"Which one?" asked John.

"The one that hit Tom on the nose," said Anne.

Footballers are today's heroes. It is very exciting when a team from a small town beats a famous club. In 1969 Swindon from the Third Division beat the First Division team Arsenal, and their victory was a great surprise. When they arrived home, thousands of supporters greeted them.

A top footballer is worth a lot of money to his club.

# 2:7 A Holiday in the Lake District

**bed and breakfast** /'bed n 'brekfəst/— The sign BED & BREAKFAST outside a house means that you can sleep there and have breakfast for a fixed payment.

**belt** /belt/ long piece of leather (etc.) that holds your trousers up. *The girl wore a belt of the latest style round her middle.*

**blanket** /'blæŋkit/ square piece of warm cloth for a bed. *He likes three blankets on his bed in winter.*

**book** /buk/ ask somebody to keep a place (a seat, a hotel room etc.) by writing one's name down. *I want to book a single room at this hotel for the night of 6 January.*

**cliff** /klif/ place where the ground falls straight down. *Your first sight of England will be the white cliffs of Dover.*

**extra** /'ekstrə/ added. *Bed and breakfast is £1; a hot bath is extra.*

**hostel** /'hɔstl/ house where people can sleep; a *youth hostel* has beds for young people on holidays etc. *Youth Hostels are marked with a red △ on the map.*

**landlady** /'lænleidi/ woman who owns a house; other people pay to sleep in her house. *Landladies often give you breakfast but no other meals.*

**path** /pɑːθ/ narrow way for people to walk along. *The path from here to the river is shorter than the road.*

**pillow** /'piləu/ bag of feathers (etc.) to go under your head in bed. *Do you like one pillow or two?*

**rescue** /'reskjuː/ help in great trouble; save. *Fireman rescued the children from the top of the burning house.*

**risk** /risk/ dangerous chance. *Take risks with your own life, not with other people's lives.*

**rope** /rəup/ long piece of something like very thick string. *There were ropes between the ship and the river bank.*

**stretch** /stretʃ/ go away into the distance *The valley began at our feet and stretched down to the lake.*

**tie** /tai/ turn one part round another to make pieces of string etc. into one. *Tie the bedclothes together to make a rope.*

**warden** /'wɔːdən/ person who looks after a hostel etc. *The warden of this youth hostel is a helpful man.*

## Bed and breakfast

JOHN (*to landlady*) I saw the bed and breakfast sign outside. I hope you're not full up. We've tried all the other houses.

LANDLADY Well, I've got a double room for the two girls. You boys can sleep on the living-room floor, if you like.

JOHN What about that shed at the bottom of the garden?

LANDLADY Yes, you can sleep there, but——

ANNE (*to landlady*) How much is it?

LANDLADY £1 bed and breakfast; extra if you want supper. It'll be a cold supper, I'm afraid—ham and salad, bread and butter—and tea, of course.

MARY Let's stop here. I'm too tired to look anywhere else.

GEORGE It's all right for you girls! You always find nice warm beds. Don't forget that *we* slept under a bridge last night.

JOHN Why didn't we bring our sleeping-bags?

GEORGE I don't like sleeping-bags. They make me sweat.

LANDLADY Please make up your minds. I can't stand here all night. It's beginning to rain.

ANNE (*to boys*) Oh, come on! A night on the floor won't hurt you.

JOHN (*to landlady*) How much do you charge for the living-room floor?

LANDLADY Half price. I'll give you blankets and pillows.

GEORGE And the shed?

LANDLADY Oh, you can sleep in the shed for nothing—but I'm afraid the pigs have to sleep there too.

---

## Exercise

**1** *Example* I'm very tired. (look in other places)
*Answer* I'm too tired to look anywhere else.

1 I'm very poor. (buy other things)
2 The hostel is very full. (take other people)
3 The landlady is very old. (do other things)
4 The rope is very short. (go in other places)
5 This warden is very kind. (send us to other places)
6 After that ham, I'm very thirsty. (eat other things)

**2** *Example* "It'll be dangerous to leave the road," said Anne.
*Answer* Anne said it would be dangerous to leave the road.

1 "It'll be nice to have an extra blanket," John said.
2 "It'll be lovely to have a nice cool salad," Anne thought.
3 "It'll be better to keep to the path," said Mary.
4 "It won't be dangerous to walk along the road," George said.
5 "It'll be terrible to sleep under a bridge again," said George.
6 "It'll be all right to go down the cliff," John thought.

## "Are you Sure?"

John and Anne, and their friends George and Mary, had spent the day on one of the loneliest mountains in the Lake District. They reached the valley again in the evening. They were hot and tired, and their feet were burning. The road stretched ahead of them down the long valley.

George stopped and pointed at the map. "Here's the Youth Hostel," he said. "It's at the bottom of this valley, not far from the lake."

"How many more miles?" asked Anne.

"Two miles to the lake and another mile from there," George answered.

"That's too far," cried Anne, "I've had enough."

"There's another way," said John. "We can leave the road here and climb over the hill. Then we'll get to the hostel in half the time."

Anne said it would be dangerous because of the rocks. Mary said she was frightened of the sheep. There were sheep everywhere on the green hillside.

"Sheep aren't dangerous, stupid!" said John.

"Yes, they are," said Mary. "A sheep bit me once."

But at last they all agreed. The climb up the hill was hard, but there was a wonderful view from the top. On every side blue mountains stretched away into the distance. Below them they could see the dark lake. But they could not see the hostel.

"Are you sure we've come the right way?" asked Anne.

"Yes," said John. "The hostel is in the middle of those trees."

"I'm glad we've booked," said Anne. "All the hostels are full."

"I'll race you to the bottom," John said to George.

"All right." They began to run. George ran down a path. But John decided to go straight down the hillside.

"Be careful," cried Anne. "There's a cliff half-way down."

John soon reached the cliff. It was more than twenty feet to the bottom. But he was sure that he could get there; there were steps in the rock. He had only got about half-way when suddenly the steps stopped. He looked down. It was too far to jump. But when he tried to climb to the top again he could not do that either. So George and the girls had to come to his help. They tied their belts together and tried to pull him up. They could not move him and one of the belts broke.

"You stay with him," George said to the girls, "while I run to the hostel for help."

The Warden and some climbers came out with ropes and a ladder and soon rescued John. But it was dark when they reached the hostel. The warden was very angry with John.

"Don't take such risks in future," he said. Then he looked at his book. "You booked for *next* Monday, not this Monday! We're full up. The girls can stay, but you boys will have to walk on to the village—three miles down the road."

This youth hostel is 1,000 feet up Coniston Old Man, a famous mountain in the southern part of the Lake District. The youth hostel has a fine view of Lake Coniston. the Youth Hostels Association buys old buildings like this one. They are often a long way from a town or village.

Keswick is one of the largest towns in the Lake District. The streets are very narrow. Cars may not stop in the street in this picture. You can see that from the yellow line along the kerb.

# 3

# A FIRST JOB

# 3:1 At the Post Office

**counter** /'kauntə/ long table in a shop or post office. *The clerks stand behind the counter; people put their money on the counter.*

**customer** /'kʌstəmə/ person who buys something in a shop etc. *People who come into the post office for stamps are customers.*

**department** /di'pɑ:tmənt/ one of the parts of the government or of a large office or shop etc. *She works in the accounts department of a big office.*

**family allowance** /'fæmili ə'lauəns/ money received from the government for the number of children in a family. *She goes to the post office every week to get her family allowance.*

**fine** /fain/ money that a person must pay because he has done wrong. *I was caught speeding and I had to pay a big fine. I was fined £15.*

**licence** /'laisəns/ piece of paper to show that a person has the right to use something. *You must have a licence for a car, a dog, or a television set.*

**manager** /'mænidʒə/ head man in an office, shop etc. *Angry customers often want to see the manager.*

**post** /pəust/ carrying letters and parcels from one place to another; put letters in a post box or take parcels to a *post office. I posted the letter yesterday, so it's in the post.*

**postal order** /'pəustl ɔ:də/ piece of paper with an order from one post office to any other post office to pay money. *A postal order for 25p costs 27½p.*

**queue** /kju:/ line of people waiting one behind the other. *There is a queue at the bus-stop. Please queue here for the No. 15 bus.*

**training** /'treiniŋ/ preparing for work by giving or receiving lessons. *A soldier needs training; a doctor's training is different.*

**Could you please . . .**
**Will you please . . .**
**Would you please . . .**
Three polite ways of asking somebody to do something. They all mean "Please".

## "It's very easy."

OLD LADY I want a 50p book of stamps, three air mail letters, a 25p postal order, a radio and television licence, and five dog licences—I'm so sorry, I mean a 25p book of stamps and *six* dog licences——

SIMON Will you please take the forms to the table over there. You can't fill them in here because a lot of people are waiting.

OLD LADY These nasty forms! What do I have to do?

SIMON It's very easy. You just write your name and address here——

OLD LADY I've forgotten my glasses. Could you please do it for me?

SIMON I'm sorry, madam, but I'm very busy. We shut at six.

OLD LADY Oh dear! Do you really shut at six o'clock? What's the time now?

SIMON It's five to. Please take the forms——

OLD LADY Do you mean the forms on the counter, or——

ANGRY CUSTOMER Would you please hurry up. I've got a train to catch.

OLD LADY Have you? I'm so sorry. Then just give me my book of stamps and my postal order. I'll come back for the licences tomorrow.

SIMON That'll be 57½p, please.

OLD LADY Oh dear! What shall I do? I've left all my money at home.

---

## Exercise

**1** *Example* Do you shut at six o'clock? (really)
*Answer* Do you really shut at six o'clock?

1 Does she want a postal order? (really)
2 Do you want to buy some stamps? (tonight)
3 Can you get a car licence at a post office? (always)
4 Will the old lady get her pension? (tomorrow)
5 Do you want to post your letters? (early)
6 Did the old lady drive Simon mad? (almost)

**2** *Example* I want to catch a train.
*Answer* I've got a train to catch.

1 I want to post a letter.
2 The old lady has to fill in a form.
3 You have to serve some customers.
4 Simon has got to serve a customer.
5 The clerks are going to pay out some family allowances.
6 I've got to get a television licence.

## Simon's first day

Simon will never forget his first day at work. The post office opened at 8.30.

"Who will be my first customer?" he wondered. He had just finished his training, and he was very anxious to do well.

Simon's first customer wanted a television licence. He gave her a dog licence form instead. Next a mother with five children asked for her family allowance. This was difficult. Simon could not remember the allowances for five and had to look in a book. It took nearly two minutes. Already there was a queue. At last he gave the woman the money. But at that moment there was a loud noise and a man said angrily, "Madam, I was here before you!"

"No, you weren't," the woman said. But the man pushed past her and came up to the counter. He was large and had a red face and a sharp nose.

"Telegram to Parramatta—fourteen words. Parcel to Rotorua—one pound two ounces," said the red-faced man. "How much will that come to?"

"Parra—?" Simon began.

"Australia!" said the red-faced man angrily.

"Rot— did you say?" Simon went on. "I'm afraid——"

"Didn't they teach you anything at school?" cried the man. "Rotorua is in New Zealand." Simon looked for the costs in his books. "Hurry up, boy!" cried the man. "I can't wait all day."

Simon tried to add up quickly. "That'll be £2," he said at last.

"No, it won't!" shouted the red-faced man. "It's £1. You are trying to steal a pound from me. Get the manager at once."

"I'm sorry, sir, I meant £1."

"Get the manager!"

Simon looked for the manager but he was not in his office.

"I'll write to him," the man said. "Young people today don't take enough care. They must learn. When I was young, I didn't make 'mistakes' like that."

Next the red-faced man said that he wanted a new car licence. Simon asked for his old licence.

"Oh," Simon said, as soon as he saw it. "I'm very sorry, but this licence finished on 30th September—a month ago. The post office can't give you a new licence now. You're four weeks too late. You'll have to write to the Motor Tax Department in the city."

"What!" cried the red-faced man.

"I'm afraid that's the law," Simon said. "I must warn you about another thing, too, sir. If the police catch you without a licence you'll have to pay a heavy fine. You'd better leave your car and walk home."

In villages the Post Office is very small. It is often part of a shop which sells sweets or newspapers. It sells stamps and receives parcels for only one or two hours a day.

In towns and cities the Post Office gives many other services. For example, it pays pensions, issues licences for cars, televisions, radios and even dogs. Money can also be paid into the Post Office Savings Bank. Of course, you can make a telephone call from any large Post Office. Telephone calls to many parts of the world go through the Post Office Tower in London by radio telephone.

# 3:2 At the Hairdresser's

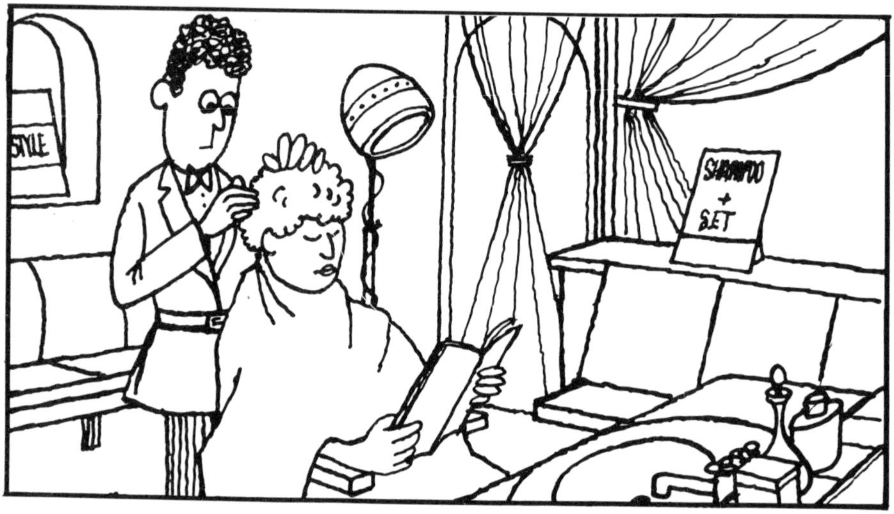


**basin** /'beisn/ thing to hold the water in which we wash our hands etc. *You can mix hot and cold water in the basin.*

**bleach** /bliːtʃ/ make (something) white or very light in colour; mixture to do this. *Her hair is dark but she bleaches it. She uses a special bleach to make her hair gold.*

**cape** /keip/ piece of cloth to go round the neck and over the shoulders. *The cape protects your dress when you have a shampoo.*

**dye** /dai/ you use a dye to change the colour of something. *Why did she use a green hair dye?*

**hairdresser** /'hɛədresə/ person who attends to customers' hair. *At the hairdresser's I always ask for Mr Charles, but Miss Annette is a clever hairdresser too.*

**happen** /'hæpn/ come by chance. *"You're late. What happened?"—"I lost my way."*

**job** /dʒɔb/ work; a piece of work. *Mr Pink gave Brenda a job in his salon. One of her jobs was to mix things for hair dye.*

**mixture** /'mikstʃə/ things mixed together. *The medicine was a nasty mixture.*

**owner** /'əunə/ person something belongs to. *That car belongs to me; I am the owner of the car.*

**rinse** /rins/ use clean water to take the soap out of something. *Wash these stockings in warm water and then rinse them in cold water.*

**salon** /'sælɔn/ (French) word for a shop, used by hairdressers, dressmakers etc. *Jane's hairdressing shop is very small and dark, but she calls it a salon, of course.*

**shampoo** /ʃæm'puː/ wash (a person's hair). *I always shampoo my own hair. I buy the shampoo at the village shop.*

**smart** /smɑːt/ well-dressed and rich-looking. *She looked very smart in her new fur coat with her snakeskin shoes and bag.*

**style** /stail/ way of doing something. *Have you seen Elizabeth Taylor's new hair style?*

**tie** /tai/ make (cloth, string etc.) meet and turn the ends together. *You tie string round a parcel.*

**trim** /trim/ make tidy by cutting. *Brenda trimmed my hair very well. I had asked for a trim, shampoo and set.*

**How about . . . ?** What do you think of . . . ? Do you like . . . ? etc. Use this when you have finished a job: *"How about that? Do you like the way I have done it?"*

## Lovely Hair

GIRL CUSTOMER Don't cut too much off, will you? My boy-friend will get angry if you do.

BRENDA My boy-friend doesn't like short hair either. . . . How about that?

GIRL CUSTOMER That's fine. Now will you please give me a cream bleach.

BRENDA I hope you'll excuse the question, but—you haven't just been ill, have you?

GIRL CUSTOMER What a strange question. Why do you ask?

BRENDA A terrible thing happened to me once. I had a young customer with beautiful long hair. It came right down to her shoulders. She asked for a cream bleach, and——

GIRL CUSTOMER Do you mean—she died?

BRENDA It was worse than that!

GIRL CUSTOMER No! Really?

BRENDA Yes! She had just come out of hospital. I shall never forget it——

GIRL CUSTOMER Go on. What happened?

BRENDA I was brushing the cream into her hair. It was really lovely hair. It——

GIRL CUSTOMER Yes? Yes?

BRENDA Suddenly her hair began to fall out. It filled the basin. I rinsed it very carefully; then I trimmed it. But she had lost so much hair that I had to give her a new style. When I had finished, it was shorter than her boy-friend's.

---

## Exercise

**1** *Example* I finished. It was shorter than her boy-friend's then.
*Answer* When I had finished, it was shorter than her boy-friend's.

1 I put the dye on. Her hair was bright green then.
2 Mr Pink cut my hair. I had a new style then.
3 She shampooed her hair with Superpong. It was very beautiful then.
4 Brenda trimmed my hair. It was tidier then.
5 The men painted the salon. It was smarter then.
6 The hairdresser rinsed her hair. It was a different colour then.

**2** *Example* She lost too much hair. I had to give her a new hair style.
*Answer* She had lost so much hair that I had to give her a new hair style.

1 The hairdresser used too much bleach. Her hair was nearly white.
2 She ordered too many bottles of shampoo. She could not pay for them.
3 They've been to too many salons. They did not remember all of them.
4 We put too much water in the basin. It came over the top.
5 We added too many colours to the mixture. It wasn't beautiful.
6 She put on too much jewellery. She wasn't really smart.

# Just a trim

PAMELA'S was a small hairdressing salon in a country town. Brenda had been working there for six weeks. She was doing well, and Mr Pink, the owner, was pleased with her. Then one morning a very smart woman came into the salon. She was about fifty and had bright golden hair.

"Good Heavens!" said Mr Pink. "That's Lady Snelgar. She usually goes to Manolo's in London."

Mr Pink hurried forward. "What can I do for you, my lady?" he said.

"I want somebody to do my hair at once," said Lady Snelgar.

"I'm terribly sorry, my lady," answered Mr Pink, "but we're all busy at the moment. Could you come back in half an hour?"

"No!" said Lady Snelgar. "I'm in a hurry." Then suddenly she noticed Brenda. Brenda was standing by an empty chair. "What about that girl?" said Lady Snelgar. "She isn't doing anything."

"Well, my lady," Mr Pink began, "Brenda is very good, but she's new, and——"

But Lady Snelgar had already taken off her coat and was sitting in the chair.

"Very well, Brenda," Mr Pink said. "Please look after Lady Snelgar."

Brenda was a little frightened, but rather proud. She tied the cape round Lady Snelgar's shoulders. "A style cut, my lady?" she asked.

"No, just a trim," answered Lady Snelgar. Brenda picked up the scissors and began to cut. She did a good job, but Lady Snelgar said nothing. Instead she handed Brenda a piece of paper which had numbers on it. "These are the colours that Mr Manolo always mixes for my hair," she said. "Be sure that the mixture is exactly right."

Brenda mixed the dye creams carefully. But Lady Snelgar called her several times. "I have to catch a train," she said. So Brenda did not have time to check the mixture.

She washed Lady Snelgar's hair, then she brushed in the dye cream. Suddenly she dropped her brush. "Excuse me, m—m—my lady," she said, "but did you really want this colour?"

Lady Snelgar looked in the glass and jumped up. Her face turned white, then red. "You STUPID girl," she cried. "Do you really imagine that I want *green* hair?"

Lady Snelgar missed her train, and Mr Pink missed his lunch. It took him a long time to wash away the green dye. When he had finished at last, he took Mr Manolo's piece of paper and studied it. Suddenly he smiled.

"I'm *very* sorry, my lady. You've had a terrible afternoon. But I'm afraid it was Mr Manolo's mistake, not Brenda's. You see, he has given you the numbers for the wrong hair dye. This must be the dye that he uses for Babs Minette, the dancer. She always wears green hair, and everybody knows that she's one of Manolo's most famous customers."

Today a woman spends as much time on her hair as on her clothes. In London hairdressers become famous as their styles become popular. Competition hairstyles may not be useful to the housewife, but who means them to be? Men too, are spending more time and money at the hairdressers as men's hair becomes longer.

# 3:3 At the Printer's

**boss** /bɔs/ owner or head of a company etc. *Mr Pink is Brenda's boss.*

**chase** /tʃeis/ frame for type. *The printer locks the type for several pages in the chase before it goes on the printing machine.*

**compartment** /kəm'pɑːtmənt/ box-like part. *Cupboards sometimes have compartments for different things.*

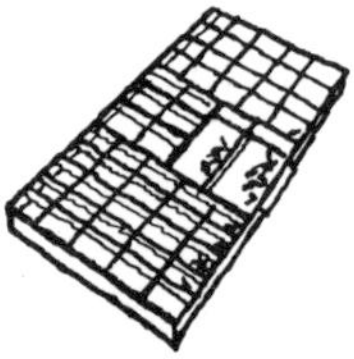

**compose** /kəm'pəuz/ put together. *The typesetter composes his type in a small frame which is called a composing stick.*

**copy** /'kɔpi/ one thing made exactly the same as another. *We printed 500 copies of the programme.*

**foreman** /'fɔːmən/ head man in a *workshop* (see below). *The foreman divides the work between the men in his group.*

**galley** /'gæli/ long frame for type from the composing stick. *We move type from the composing stick first to galleys and later to a chase.*

**machine-minder** /mə'ʃiːnmaində/ person who works a machine and watches it. *The machine-minder puts the chase into the machine.*

**mirror** /'mirə/ looking-glass, piece of glass in which you can see your own face. *Watch the car behind you in your driving mirror.*

**programme** /'prəugræm/ list of things that people will do. *Theatre programmes are expensive.*

**proof** /pruːf/ first printing, made to correct mistakes. *Check the galley proofs very carefully and mark the mistakes clearly.*

**punctuation marks** /pʌŋktju'eiʃn mɑːks/ stops like " , " ' ; ' . *Don't forget the punctuation marks when you write in English.*

**type** /taip/ small pieces of metal to print letters, numbers etc. *Each piece of type prints one letter.*

**typesetter** /'taipsetə/ worker who puts type into the frame for the printer. *A man needs a lot of experience to become a good typesetter.*

**typewriter** /'taipraitə/ machine used in an office to write letters etc. *Put a piece of paper in the typewriter and type a letter.*

**upside-down** /'ʌpsaid'daun/ with the top at the bottom. *This is printed upside-down.* (printed upside-down)

**workshop** /'wəːkʃɔp/ building in which people work with machines. *My car is in the workshop for repairs.*

## "Can I try?"

TYPESETTER So you want to be a typesetter, do you?

BOB Yes, I'd like to. What's in this big case? The type?

TYPESETTER Yes. You'll find all the letters, numbers and punctuation marks in it. It has got more than 100 compartments.

BOB Why is this compartment bigger than all the others?

TYPESETTER It's the compartment for the "e"s. There are more "e"s in the English language than any other letter. Look. This is a composing stick. We set the type in it. Pick it up and read the first line.

BOB "Lady Pons——" It's difficult. It's exactly like the type on a typewriter.

TYPESETTER Now hold it in front of that mirror and read it.

BOB "Lady Ponsonby invites you to a party in the village hall." Oh, I see! Can I try to set some type?

TYPESETTER Of course. Take the composing stick and set these two lines. Call me when you're ready.

BOB (*a quarter of an hour later*) I've finished. I've checked it several times.

TYPESETTER (*looks at stick*) Fine! You're learning very quickly. But you've made one small mistake. To print a line, you must begin on the left. Then you put the type *backwards* in the stick from left to right. You have worked from left to right, but you haven't put the letters in backwards. Therefore if we print these two lines in the printing-machine, the letters will come out upside-down.

---

## Exercise

**1** *Example* "You've made one small mistake, Bob," the typesetter said.
*Answer* The typesetter told Bob that he had made one small mistake.

1 "You've worked from left to right, Bob," the foreman said.
2 "We haven't really got time," the foreman said to the boss.
3 "I want my dinner," the foreman said several times to Bob.
4 "I haven't finished it yet," Bob told the foreman.
5 "I want you to check the list, Bob," the boss said.
6 "I've locked the type in the chase," Bob said to the machine-minder.

**2** *Example* Somebody checked the galley proofs very carefully.
*Answer* The galley proofs were very carefully checked.

1 The printer's men set the invitations very easily.
2 Somebody put in the punctuation marks very carefully.
3 Somebody dropped the chase on the galley very stupidly.
4 They set the type very soon.
5 Somebody printed the programmes very quickly.
6 They printed 500 copies very soon.

## A rush job

Bob had been at the printer's for about a week. He had set type for addresses and telephone numbers, bills and things like that. He enjoyed the work. One day the boss hurried into the workshop.

"Here's a rush job, Jack," he said to the foreman. "It's not very long, but it's in Czech."

A large group of Czech school children were staying in the college in the town. They did not understand English very well yet. So the Czech teacher had decided to translate their work programme into their own language.

The programme was not very long—just a list of dates and times and a few words on each line. The foreman said that it would fill one page.

"They want 500 copies," said the boss.

"We haven't really got time," answered the foreman. "We've got this other rush job—150 invitation cards for Lady Garnett's garden party. Of course I could give this Czech job to Bob. He hasn't had much experience, but he studied languages at school."

The boss agreed. Bob looked at the programme. He had learnt French and German at school, but Czech was not at all like French *or* German. He could not even guess the meaning of the words.

He began to set the lines in his composing stick. It was a long and difficult job.

There were a lot of figures on the page. At first Bob used the wrong type for the figures. Half-way through the work, he saw his mistake. He had to change all the numbers.

"Hurry up!" the foreman said several times. "I want my dinner!"

At last Bob had put all the lines on the galley. He printed a galley proof and began to check it. Suddenly the foreman came up to him.

"Good!" he said. "The page is ready for the chase, is it?"

Before Bob could say, "No, not yet," the foreman picked up the galley and put the page of type in the chase.

"Take the chase to the machine," he said.

"But I haven't finished——" Bob began.

The foreman was not listening. He had gone back to Lady Garnett's invitation cards. "Be quick," he said. "I'll want to use the machine soon."

Bob took the chase to the machine and handed it to the machine-minder. The machine-minder pushed the page of type into the machine and printed the 500 copies. But when the Czech teacher received his programme, he was angry. Bob had mixed some of the figures.

"What!" cried the teacher. "Supper—8.00! Breakfast—14.00! Walk in the country—22.30! My pupils will think that the English are mad!"

The famous morning newspaper, The Times, is printed in this room. The men are checking the proofs before they send some of the papers in vans to London. The rest of the papers are sent by train, sea and air to other parts of Great Britain and the world.

520,000 papers are printed every night between 5 p.m. and 9 p.m. except Saturday night. A Sunday newspaper—The Observer—is printed on the machines on Saturday night.

The second picture is an interesting view of a printing-machine. It was built especially for Her Majesty's Stationery Office to print telephone books. H.M.S.O. prints all the telephone books for Great Britain on twelve machines but the City of Hull has its own telephone service and prints its own books.

# 3:4 A Photographic Shop

**button** /ˈbʌtn/ small *knob* (see below); the round thing that goes through a *buttonhole* to bring two parts of a coat, shirt etc. together.

**contact print** /ˈkɔntækt print/ photograph made by letting light through a negative (see below) when the negative is touching (in contact with) the paper. *If you want a picture larger than a contact print, you ask for an enlargement.*

**experienced** /iksˈpiəriənst/ having experience. *An experienced driver doesn't make a sudden turn on a wet road.*

**exposure** /iksˈpəuʒə/ length of time when light can reach the film. *The fastest exposure on this camera is one hundredth of a second. This film allows thirty-six exposures.*

**focus** /ˈfəukəs/ move the lens (see below) to suit the distance of the thing one wants to photograph. *Focus on the group under the tree over there. Now change the focus to twenty feet.*

**knob** /nɔb/ round thing to turn, pull or press. *The door isn't locked; just turn the knob.*

**lens** /lenz/ piece of glass of a special shape that makes a thing look larger or smaller. *The lenses of her glasses are very thick; she is very short-sighted.*

**negative** /ˈnegətiv/ black-and-white film, black where the subject was light etc.

**photograph** /ˈfəutəgrɑːf/ picture made with a camera; *photo* is a short form. *He is a good photographer; he has taken some lovely photographs of the river.*

**shutter** /ˈʃʌtə/ part of the camera that opens to allow light to pass through the lens. *This camera has a fast shutter with speeds up to one five-hundredth of a second.*

**simple** /ˈsimpl/ easy to use. *It's a simple camera with only two knobs.*

**slide** /slaid/ photograph to show with light behind it. *I have a special machine which throws the pictures from my slides on a large sheet.*

**snap** /snæp/ photograph taken quickly. *Are you tired of other people's holiday snaps?*

**stick, stuck** /stik stʌk/ become fixed. *Cold eggs stick to dishes. I can't get the key out; it's stuck.*

**view-finder** /ˈvjuːfaində/ eye-piece to see the picture as it will be in the photograph. *You can't see anything if you put your finger over the view-finder.*

**winding knob** /ˈwaindiŋ nɔb/ knob to move the film in the camera.

## Jim sells a camera

GIRL CUSTOMER I want to buy a camera. What kind do you recommend?

JIM Well, how much money do you want to spend?

GIRL CUSTOMER I want something cheap.

JIM Are you an experienced photographer?

GIRL CUSTOMER I've had no experience at all.

JIM What kind of photographs are you going to take?

GIRL CUSTOMER Oh, you know—family snaps, holiday scenes, colour slides——

JIM Here's a camera that would suit you very well. It's got a very good lens, and it costs only £5.

GIRL CUSTOMER No, not that one. It's *such* an ugly colour, and there are too many knobs on it. I want something very simple. I've never taken a photograph before, you see.

JIM Then I would recommend a box camera. You can't make mistakes with box cameras. There's no trouble about focusing or exposures. You just look in the view-finder and press the button.

GIRL CUSTOMER Can I try?

JIM Of course. Here's the camera. Imagine that you're taking a photo of me.

GIRL CUSTOMER Like this?

JIM Well, not quite.

GIRL CUSTOMER Why? What am I doing wrong?

JIM You've got your left hand in front of the shutter.

---

## Exercise

**1** *Example* That camera is very expensive. (cheap)
*Answer* That camera is too expensive. I want something cheap.

1 That camera has very many knobs. (simple)
2 That material is very ugly. (beautiful)
3 That shutter is very slow. (fast)
4 This camera is very old. (new)
5 This exercise is very easy. (difficult)
6 That camera is very old-fashioned. (modern)

**2** *Example* That camera is an ugly colour.
*Answer* I don't like that camera. It's such an ugly colour.

1 That camera has a bad lens.
2 This photographer is a stupid man.
3 This view-finder is a poor thing.
4 The shutter is a slow one.
5 This camera has a small rewind knob.
6 That photographic shop has a poor light.

## Pictures of birds

One morning a young man in narrow trousers and a bright blue shirt came into the camera shop. A moment later a lady in a brown suit pushed past him and put a camera down on the counter.

"There's a film in the camera," she told Jim, "but we can't get it out because the winding knob has stuck."

Jim looked at the lady and then at the young man in the bright shirt. "We, madam?" he asked. "Are you together then?"

"No," said the lady. "I meant my husband."

"Then I'm afraid I must serve this gentleman first. He arrived before you. I'm very sorry, madam."

"But I'm in a great hurry——" the lady began.

"Please serve the lady," the young man said with a smile. "I can wait."

Jim took the camera into the darkroom, took out the film and hurried back to the shop. He put the film down on the counter and pointed to the camera.

"The knob is broken," he told the lady. "Shall I order a new one for you?"

"I'll ask my husband," the lady said. "It's his camera. Meanwhile please be very careful with the film. The photographs are very special, and my husband will be very angry if anything happens to them. He wants to use them in a wild-life book that he's writing."

"Do you want contact prints, madam?" Jim asked.

The lady said "yes", and Jim wrote the order down in his book.

"They'll be ready on Monday." he said.

"Good!" said the lady, and walked out of the shop.

Before Jim could pick up the lady's film, the young man put *his* film down on the counter and said with a smile, "My photographs are very special too. You'll agree when you see them. Contact prints for me, too, and please post them to this address."

He handed Jim a piece of paper and then left. When Jim had written the order in his book, he picked up the two films——

On Tuesday morning early the lady came to collect her husband's prints. Jim handed her an envelope. She was in a hurry again, and she left as soon as she had paid. An hour later a man rushed into the shop and threw the same envelope on the counter.

"You gave my wife the wrong prints!" he cried.

He was very angry indeed. At the same time the young man rushed in. He too threw an envelope on the counter.

"These aren't *my* prints!" he cried. "It's true that I took photographs of birds during my holiday. But my birds wore swim-suits—not feathers!"

Photography became cheap and popular at the end of the last century. One of these pictures shows a "while-u-wait" photographer at work in the early 1900's. The other shows a modern studio with lights and a screen for the background. Colour film and movie cameras are now cheap enough for everyone to buy.

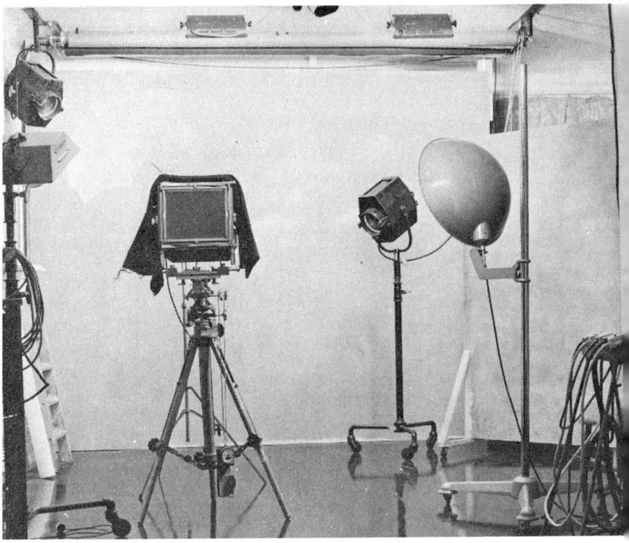

# 3:5 Window-dressing

**arrange** /ə'reindʒ/ put in a special order. *You have arranged the display in this window very well; I like the arrangement.*

**in charge** /in 'tʃɑːdʒ/—The person who is *in charge* gives orders to the others.

**display** /dis'plei/ show. *A big shop window is sometimes called a display window.*

**dummy** /'dʌmi/ figure like a person. *Shop window dummies are thinner than most of us.*

**fire** /'faiə/ tell somebody that he (or she) has lost his job. *Miss Spratt fired Susan, but then the management fired Miss Spratt.*

**jersey** /'dʒəːzi/ warm piece of clothing for men, women or children. *In a game of football all the players of one side wear jerseys of the same colour.*

**management** /'mænidʒmənt/ persons who have a company or look after it. *The management of a big store gives its orders to a manager* (man) *or manageress* (woman).

**notice** /'nəutis/ warning before one stops work. *Susan can give a week's notice and leave the job after seven days. If Miss Spratt fires Susan without notice, she has to give her seven days' pay.*

**reference** /'refrəns/ letter to recommend a person for a job. *We gave him the job because he had very good references.*

**skating** /'skeitiŋ/ moving on ice by using boots with *skates* of steel. *People in the north of Europe like skating in winter.*

**strike** /straik/ stop work until there is agreement about pay, hours etc. *The men are striking for more pay; they're on strike. The strike will go on until they get more pay.*

**waste** /weist/ use up without doing good; lose by not using carefully. *Work hard; don't waste your time. Cut the cloth carefully and don't waste any.*

**whistle** /'wisl/ small instrument used by a policeman; its loud sound makes people look at him. *A policeman used to use his whistle to call for help, but today he does that with a pocket radio.*

**window-dresser** /'windəudresə/ person who arranges the display in a shop window. *Window-dressers work in shop windows.*

## "That woman makes me sick!"

MANAGERESS Susan, I saw you smiling at a young man through the window. Who was it?

SUSAN I didn't smile at a young man. I didn't smile at anybody. I was too busy.

MANAGERESS Busy, were you? Well, you did a very bad job. I told you to put the nylon dresses on the right and the cotton dresses on the left.

SUSAN Excuse me, Miss Spratt, but you didn't. You told me to put the nylon dresses on the left and the cotton dresses on the right. I wrote everything down in my notebook. Look.

MANAGERESS I don't want to see it. I'm not pleased with your work. You've broken an arm of one of the dummies.

SUSAN It was broken already. I reported it—you know I did!

MANAGERESS Don't talk to me like that! Get back to your work. You're wasting my time. (*She goes away.*)

SHOP GIRL That woman makes me sick. She's never pleased with anybody. She'll soon lose all her girls. How many left last week? Three, wasn't it?

SUSAN Yes, and if she goes on like this, I'll give notice too.

SHOP GIRL Why don't we all go on strike?

SUSAN A good idea! Let's start tomorrow.

SHOP GIRL Well, I'd rather wait until next month.

SUSAN Why?

SHOP GIRL Because I'm starting my holiday tomorrow.

---

## Exercise

**1** *Example* I reported the broken dummy.
*Answer* I reported it—you know I did!

1 She has finished the work.
2 We arranged the display.
3 He'll mend the dummy.
4 You're wasting your time.
5 They've lost the blouse.
6 I'm doing a good job.

**2** *Example* You were smiling at a young man. I saw you.
*Answer* I saw you smiling at a young man.

1 I was arranging the dummies. The manageress saw me.
2 They were wasting time. The manager heard them.
3 He was walking past the window. The window-dresser saw him.
4 Susan was planning a display. The manageress found her.
5 The woman was stealing nylons. The shop girl caught her.
6 We were skating on the lake. The owner saw us.

## The big window

One morning Miss Spratt stopped Susan while she was carrying some dresses to the window.

"Susan, your work is still very bad," she said.

"What have I done now, Miss Spratt?" said Susan.

"You talk to the other shop girls too much and you're not polite when you speak to me."

"But Miss Spratt——" Susan began.

"No!" said Miss Spratt. "I've had enough. You'll have to find another job. I'll give you until Saturday, but don't ask me for a reference. I wouldn't recommend you to anybody."

Susan did not say anything, but she was so angry that she dropped all the dresses on the floor. Two shop girls who had heard Miss Spratt helped to pick them up. "That woman!" one of them cried. "She'll never find a better window-dresser than you."

"Don't worry," said Susan. "I'll teach her a lesson before I leave. Tell all your friends to take a walk past the big window during the lunch-hour tomorrow. I'll prepare a little surprise for them."

The next day, as soon as Miss Spratt went out to lunch, Susan rushed to the big window. It was full of dummies. There were dummies of big men and dummies of pretty girls. The men were wearing narrow trousers and open-neck shirts. The girls were wearing light summer dresses. A big notice said: "DRESS FOR THE HOLIDAYS AT GAGE'S". Susan had arranged this holiday scene and she was very proud of it.

She looked around her. On her right stood a "girl" dummy with long golden hair. On her left stood a tall "young man" with blue eyes. Quickly she dressed the young man in a short skating skirt and a little pink blouse. Then she dressed the girl in football shorts, football boots and a red jersey.

At once people began to stop outside the window. They laughed and pushed. Soon the street was full of people and a policeman arrived and blew his whistle.

At 2 o'clock Miss Spratt returned. She saw Susan's display and almost died of anger. "You'll leave now!" she cried. "AT ONCE!"

But the same afternoon the management heard the full story. They did not want to lose any more girls. So they fired Miss Spratt.

Susan went to London and found a window-dressing job in a big West End store. The manageress liked Susan's displays. In fact these displays soon became well known. Susan even won a window-dressing competition and got a free trip to Paris.

Then one day the manageress called Susan to her office. "You're too busy, my dear," she said. "You need help. I've borrowed a woman from another department. She says that she has had some experience of window-dressing. But of course you will be in charge. You'd better have a talk with her."

A moment later the door opened—and Miss Spratt walked in!

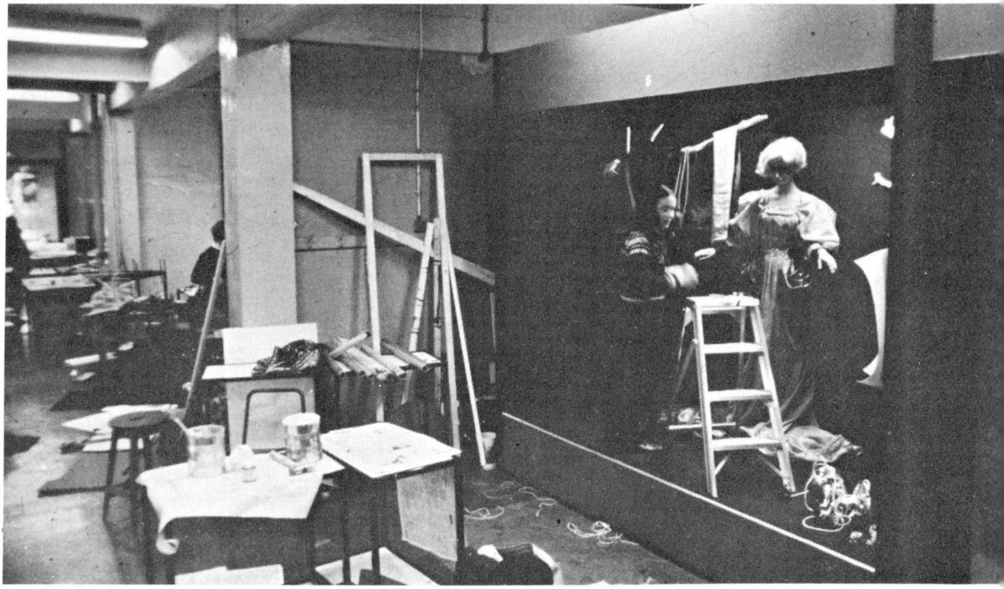

When people see an exciting window display they want to buy from the shop. The work of a window-dresser is to bring the customers in. There are now special courses in London which train window-dressers. The training teaches them how to use colour, movement and surprise. It also shows them how to make use of one idea for several windows.

# 3:6 In the Office

**all right** /'ɔːl 'rait/ without trouble. *Famous last words: "It's all right. We can cross the road here."*

**business** /'biznis/ work which needs an office; getting money by buying and selling etc. *Mr Peck is a business man. Peck's is not a big business.*

**chief clerk** /'tʃiːf'klɑːk/ head clerk in an office. *The chief clerk takes care of the work in the office.*

**correspondence** /kɔris'pɔndəns/ letters and answers to them etc. *Most big offices have a lot of correspondence with government departments.*

**dictate** /dik'teit/ say words for another person to write down. *The manager is dictating some letters to his secretary. She can take dictation at 120 words a minute.*

**filing cabinet** /'failiŋ kæbinət/ iron cupboard for *files*; files are made of card, and they hold the letters etc. about one subject (thing or idea) or one customer. *The files are arranged in alphabetical* (A, B, C) *order in the filing cabinets.*

**important** /im'pɔːtənt/ having a special place, greater than the others. *The president is the most important man in the country.*

**invoice** /'invɔis/ list of the goods that have gone to somebody, with prices. *I have received an invoice for four books, but only three books have arrived.*

**Limited (Ltd)** /'limitid/—After the name of a company this means that it is owned by more than one person.

**matter** /'mætə/ trouble. *What's the matter?* (= What is wrong?) *There's something the matter with him, he's always tired.*

**no wonder** /'nəu 'wʌndə/ it is not surprising (that . . .). *"You're a very pretty girl. No wonder he loves you."*

**owe** /əu/ have to pay money etc. (to somebody). *You owe me £5 but I can wait until next month for it. We owe our thanks to the people who have helped us.*

**receipt** /ri'siːt/ piece of paper to say that somebody has paid money. *Please pay this bill and get a receipt for the payment.*

**receiver** /ri'siːvə/ part of the telephone that we put to our ear. *Pick up the receiver and listen: when you hear the dialling tone* (Br–r–r–r), *dial the number.*

**secretary** /'sekrətri/ person (usually a girl) who does office work for somebody. *"I'm afraid Mr Peck is out. Will you speak to his secretary?"*

**shorthand** /'ʃɔːthænd/ way of writing quickly. *"Can you write shorthand?"—"Yes, I can. But I can't always read my own shorthand notes."*

**typist** /'taipist/ person (usually a girl) who uses a typewriter to write letters etc. *She is quite a good typist; she types at about sixty words a minute.*

## "How are you getting on?"

JANE It's your first day at Peck's, isn't it? How are you getting on?

JACK Well, I haven't really started work yet. I've been with Mr Snuggs, the chief clerk. He was explaining the work to me.

JANE What do you think of Mr Snuggs?

JACK He seems very kind. But he looks terribly tired. What's the matter with him?

JANE He has too much work. There aren't enough clerks or typists in the office. Poor old Snuggs has to look after the filing cabinet. Sometimes he even has to take letters to the post and open the door.

JACK But you're a clerk. Don't you help him?

JANE I do help him sometimes. But I'm usually very busy. I work in the Accounts Department. I prepare invoices, bills and receipts—and there are a lot of them. We're not a very big business, but we get a lot of correspondence.

JACK But what about Miss Snipe, the secretary?

JANE Oh her! She's no good at all. Snuggs often has to do her work too. She puts wrong addresses on envelopes. She often arrives late. Snuggs sometimes has to type her letters—and he types very badly. She can't even take dictation in shorthand.

JACK Why doesn't Mr Peck fire her?

JANE He'd like to fire her, but he can't—because of Mr Snuggs.

JACK Why not?

JANE Because he doesn't want to lose Snuggs. Snuggs is a very good chief clerk and Mr Peck is very fond of him.

JACK I don't understand.

JANE Well, you see, Mary Snipe is going to marry Mr Snuggs's son!

---

## Exercise

**1** *Example* I'm looking at Mr Snuggs. He's very tired.
*Answer* Mr Snuggs looks very tired.

1 I'm looking at my secretary. She's very busy.
2 I'm listening to the chief. He's very angry.
3 I've got some meat in my mouth. It's nice.
4 We're looking at our new filing cabinet. It's very big.
5 I'm holding the flowers to my nose. They're very sweet.
6 We're watching the motor race. It's very dangerous.

**2** *Example* Mr Snuggs—show—me—do
*Answer* Mr Snuggs has been showing me what to do.

1 The chief clerk—tell—the typist—type
2 Mr Peck—tell—his secretary—say
3 Mr Peck's secretary—show—me—do with receipts
4 He—tell—his wife—wear
5 Jack—ask—Mr Snuggs—do
6 The shorthand-typist—ask—the chief clerk—say

## The latest figures

Jack had just started work at Pecks Dried Fruit Ltd. At first he did not find the work at all interesting. Making tea seemed to be his most important job. Twice—sometimes three times—a day he had to make tea for everybody in the office. It was not easy.

"Remember that Mr Peck likes his tea without milk or sugar," said Mr Snuggs. "Miss Snipe takes milk, but no sugar. And I like a lot of milk and five lumps of sugar." Jack often forgot to give the right tea to somebody. On the third day he gave Mr Snuggs's tea to Mr Peck. Mr Peck was almost sick. "I *hate* sweet tea, boy!" he cried. "Never forget that!"

"No, sir," said Jack.

Putting correspondence and orders in the different filing cabinets soon became Jack's special job. At first he made many mistakes. "Why are there so many people called George Smith?" he wondered. There was a George Smith in Birmingham, England, and another in Birmingham, Alabama. There was one in Sydney, Australia, and another in Capetown, South Africa. Names were really a problem.

Late one morning the telephone rang. Jack was alone in the office. He picked up the receiver. A man said, "Is that Peck's Dried Fruit Limited? Mr Arkell speaking. I'm rather worried about my account. Could you please give me the latest figures?"

"Just a moment, please," said Jack.

He went to the Accounts Department and soon came back with the answer.

"You owe us £10,542, sir," he said.

"What!" cried Mr Arkell. "Will you please check that figure."

Jack went back to the Accounts Department. The figure was quite correct. Mr Arkell did not believe it. He asked at once for Mr Peck. Jack told him that Mr Peck was out at lunch.

"Well, tell him that I'm coming to see him this afternoon!" cried Mr Arkell.

Two hours later Mr Arkell walked into the front office. "Where's Mr Peck?" he cried.

Jack trembled. He took Mr Arkell to Mr Peck's office. Mr Arkell pushed past him and went straight in. Jack waited outside and listened. He heard a few angry words. Then suddenly there was a loud laugh. The door opened. Mr Arkell came out. He was still laughing.

"Don't worry, boy!" he said. "Everything is all right."

A moment later Mr Peck called Jack into his office.

"You made a stupid mistake," Mr Peck said. "We've got one customer called Mr Arkell and another called Mr R. Kell. That was Mr R. Kell. His account comes to only £150. No wonder he was angry."

People can work quickly and easily in a modern office. We have had typewriters and telephones in offices for many years, but now telex and adding machines, computers and electric typewriters make work even easier.

In a modern open-plan office, a lot of people can work together. There is light and air for everybody. The other photograph was taken in 1913. Small offices like these are now very unusual. Each year large numbers of old offices are pulled down, and new ones take their place.

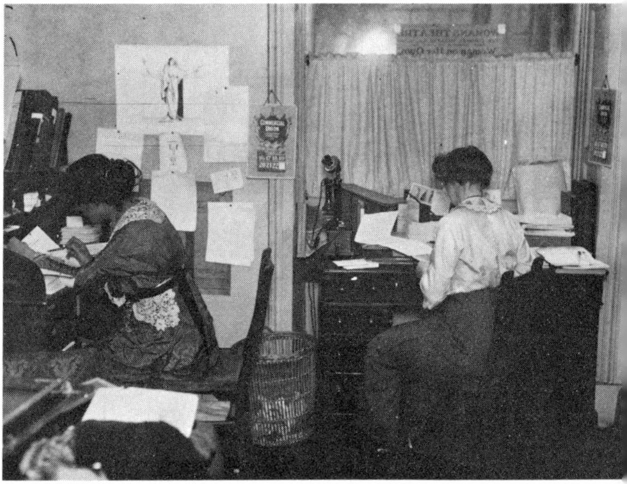

# 3:7 An Electrician

**circuit** /'sə:kit/ set of electric *wires* (see below) etc. through which a *current* (see below) travels. *There is a fuse in every circuit.*

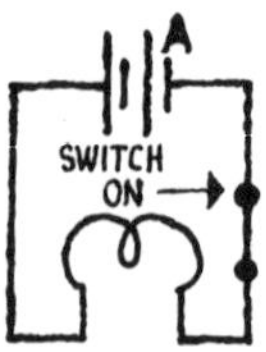


**current** /'kʌrənt/—We say that water moves down a river in a *current*; we use the same word when electricity moves along a wire—there is an *electric current* in the wire. *Turn off (switch off) the current before you try to mend an electric hair-dryer.*

**fuse** /fju:z/ piece of thin *wire* (see below); it *fuses* (= melts) if too great an electric current passes through it; this saves the lamps etc. in the circuit. *Mrs Dale has blown a fuse again. She says, "I have fused the lights."*

**hair-dryer** /'hɛədraiə/ electric machine to dry a woman's hair. *In the hairdresser's you sit under a big hair-dryer.*

**inspector** /in'spektə/ man who looks at things to see that they are right. *A ticket inspector travels on this train.*

**interest** /'intrist/ catch one's attention. *This book interests me; I can't put it down and go to bed.*

**plug** /plʌg/ thing with two pins or three pins to take electric current from a point in the wall. *Modern 3-pin plugs have 13-amp fuses inside them.*

**screw** /skru:/—You hammer a nail into something, but you turn a *screw*. You turn it, or *screw* it in, with a *screwdriver*. *Turn the screwdriver clockwise to screw something up; turn it anticlockwise to unscrew a screw.*

**spark** /spɑ:k/ bright light seen when electricity jumps from one point to another. *I touched that wire with a screwdriver and there was a spark.*

**tool** /tu:l/ instrument that we use to repair a machine etc. *Hammers, screwdrivers and axes are tools.*

**torch** /tɔ:tʃ/ small electric light to carry in one hand. *"It's a very dark road. Carry a torch when you walk along it."*

**van** /væn/ car with a place for goods instead of a back seat *The electrician's van had "SPARK—ELECTRICIAN—Electrical repairs of all kinds" on the sides.*

**wire** /'waiə/ length of iron etc. like a hard string. *We use wire for fences etc. All the electric wires in a house are called the wiring of the house.*

**come round** visit a house. *Mr Spark told me to go round to Mrs Dale's house. "Telephone her first," he said, "and tell her that you are coming round."*

**drop in** visit a house without a special invitation. *Tom Jones is an old friend of the family; he drops in to see us about once a week.*

## "Well, er——"

DICK I'm sorry I'm so late, Mr Spark.
MR SPARK That's all right. Come in and sit down. Your father tells me you want to be an electrician.
DICK I'd like to. Have you got a place for me in your shop?
MR SPARK We'll see. What made you decide to be an electrician?
DICK Electrical things have always interested me.
MR SPARK I've received a good report from your school. But what do you know about electricity? Have you any experience?
DICK I can mend a fuse or repair a plug, and I've just made an electric clock for my mother.
MR SPARK Really? That's interesting. I'd like to see it.
DICK I'm afraid you can't. It's fixed to the wall.
MR SPARK Well, I live quite near you. I'll drop in tomorrow. You can show it to me then.
DICK Well, er——
MR SPARK What's the trouble?
DICK I'm afraid the clock doesn't work very well yet. It sometimes stops. That's why I was late.

---

## Exercise

**1** *Example* I decided to be an electrician.
*Answer* What made you decide to be an electrician?

1 I remembered to bring the torch.
2 She dropped her hair-dryer in the bath.
3 He turned off the current.
4 Dick forgot his tool bag.
5 They asked for some fuse wire.
6 The electrician dropped his screwdriver.

**2** *Example* Your father—you—be an electrician
*Answer* Your father tells me you want to be an electrician.

1 Mr Spark—you—mend the fuse
2 The electrician—he—drive the van
3 My wife—the electrician—change the wiring
4 Mrs Dale—her husband—use the torch
5 Your husband—you—buy a new hair-dryer
6 My father—the inspector—see my tools

## Mrs Dale's fuses

It was 5.30 on a cold winter's evening. Mr Spark had already gone home. Suddenly the telephone rang. It was Mrs Dale, one of Mr Spark's best customers. She was in great trouble. This did not surprise Dick, because Mrs Dale was very often in trouble. This time she had dropped a bread knife into an electric fire and fused all the lights.

"I can't mend fuses and my husband hasn't come home yet," she said.

"All right, madam," Dick said. "I'll come round at once." He picked up his tool bag, got into the van and drove straight to the house.

Mrs Dale was waiting for him at the front door. The house was completely dark and as cold as ice. Dick took a torch from his tool-bag.

"The fuse-box is in the garage, isn't it, madam?" he asked.

"I think it is," Mrs Dale answered. "My husband always goes there when I fuse the lights. But please be quick. We're having a party tonight. I've just washed my hair, and it's still wet."

Dick went into the garage and soon found the fuse-box. But then he had to ask for Mrs Dale's help. "Will you please hold the torch, madam?" he asked.

"Oh dear! Do you really need my help?" she said.

But she held the torch while Dick opened the fuse-box. He had just taken his screwdriver and a piece of fuse-wire from his bag when suddenly there was a loud cry. At the same time there was a crash and the torch went out. Dick knocked his head on the fuse-box and dropped his screwdriver.

"What has happened?" he asked anxiously. "Are you all right, madam?"

"A mouse!" cried Mrs Dale. "I saw a mouse!"

"A mouse won't hurt you, madam," Dick said. "Is the torch broken?" But Mrs Dale did not hear him. She was crying, "Help! Help!"

At that moment Mr Dale arrived home. He heard his wife's cries. He opened the garage doors and rushed forward.

"No!" cried Dick.

But it was too late. Mr Dale knocked Dick down. Of course Mrs Dale explained everything to her husband. Mr Dale said that he was very sorry, and Dick was able to mend the fuse without any more trouble. The lights were soon on again, Mrs Dale went upstairs, and Mr Dale invited Dick into the kitchen.

"I'll make you a cup of tea," Mr Dale said. "It's a very old house, you know. The wiring is very bad. I'm afraid that if an inspector——"

At that moment all the lights went out again. There was a loud cry from the bathroom. Mrs Dale had dropped her hair-dryer into the bath!

These men are electricians. The first man works for the Central Electricity Generating Board, a government department. Look at his rubber boots and his helmet.

The other electrician is working in a theatre. You can see the text of the play which gives him directions. He will change the stage lighting very often during the play. His job is very difficult and he must be very careful.

# 4

# THEY SERVE THE PUBLIC

# 4:1 Accident

**AA patrol car** /ˈeiˈei pəˈtrəul kɑː/ car which is always ready to help AA (Automobile Association) members and other drivers. *AA patrol cars are painted bright yellow.*

**actually** /ˈæktʃuəli/ in fact. *No, I'm not a pupil; actually I'm one of the teachers.*

**ambulance** /ˈæmbjuləns/ special long car to take people to hospital. *"Your father is very ill. Telephone for an ambulance."*

**bend** /bend/ place where the road turns to the right or the left. *"It's a dangerous bend. Drive slowly."*

**blood** /blʌd/—*A man's blood is bright red when it leaves the heart.*

**breakdown van** /ˈbreikdaun væn/ large car which can pull or lift other cars after an accident or other trouble. *If the man can't repair your car here, he'll pull it behind his breakdown van to the garage.*

**crowd** /kraud/ large number of people in one place. *There is always a crowd at the airport when a famous person arrives. Don't crowd round the injured man; give him air.*

**damaged** /ˈdæmidʒd/ broken. *"I'm sorry to say that your car is damaged. It hit a street lamp."—"Are you going to pay for the damage?"*

**ditch** /ditʃ/ deep way for water near the sides of a road. *Fields have ditches too; rainwater runs into the ditch and the ground dries quickly.*

**flash** /flæʃ/ shine brightly for a moment. *A police car uses its flashing blue light when it has to go fast.*

**happen** /ˈhæpn/ come by chance. *"You're late. What happened?"—"I missed the bus."*

**injured** /ˈindʒəd/ wounded in an accident etc. *She fell downstairs and was badly injured by the fall.*

**mirror** /ˈmirə/ looking-glass, piece of glass in which you can see your own face. *Your driving mirror shows you the road behind your car.*

**rabbit** /ˈræbit/ small animal with long ears. *There are wild rabbits in the fields, but children keep rabbits of a different kind as pets.*

**siren** /ˈsaiərən/ machine that makes a loud warning noise on police cars, ambulances etc. *If you hear a siren behind you, drive to the side of the road.*

**stretcher** /ˈstretʃə/ light bed; two men can carry a person on it, and an ambulance has a special frame for it. *Ambulance men put an injured person on a stretcher.*

## "It's happened again!"

BILL Excuse me. I'm from the *Evening Star*. You saw the accident, I imagine. Can I ask you a few questions about it?

WOMAN I should be glad to answer any questions. Yes, I saw it happen. I saw the car come round that corner.

BILL What happened exactly?

WOMAN He was driving very fast. He couldn't stop, and he drove straight into the lake.

BILL Is he—still in the car?

WOMAN Oh no! The water isn't deep. In fact he is not hurt at all—just wet. He has gone to that farmhouse over there. He's going to telephone the police and ask for a breakdown van.

BILL Why couldn't he stop? Was he on the wrong side of the road?

WOMAN Well, yes he was! It's rather a sharp bend. Of course——

BILL There's a car there—right on the bend—almost in the middle of the road. Who does it belong to?

WOMAN It belongs to me, actually. You see, there's a lovely view across the lake from that corner. So I *had* to stop!

BILL But—isn't it rather a dangerous place——?

WOMAN Ah! Here comes the police-car! They *are* driving fast!

BILL Quick! You must move your car——!

WOMAN Oh dear! It's happened again! Men drive badly, don't they? Well, good-bye. I'm sure you will be able to help those poor policemen out of the water!

---

## Exercise

**1** *Example* that car—to—does—who—belong
*Answer* Who does that car belong to?

1 about—those drivers—talking—are—what
2 the light—for—was—what—flashing
3 is—where—to—going—the breakdown van
4 by—injured—the poor man—what—was
5 did—the AA patrol car—from—come—where
6 who—some information—give—the woman—to—did

**2** *Example* The car came round that corner. I saw it.
*Answer* I saw the car come round that corner.

1 The ambulance arrived. I heard it.
2 Three cars went into the ditch. The boy saw them.
3 Those AA patrol cars came to the bend. We saw them.
4 The policemen brought a stretcher. Did you see them?
5 My son damaged my car. I didn't see him.
6 The sirens sounded. I never heard them.

## A chance for a story

Bill Pratt was driving along the Portsmouth road. Suddenly he heard the noise of a siren in the distance. The noise got louder and louder. He looked in his mirror and saw, just behind him, a car with a flashing blue light. A police car! A few moments later he heard the sound of a second siren, then a third, then a fourth, then a fifth! Another police car and three ambulances rushed past him.

"There's been an accident," Bill thought. "Here's a chance for a story."

Round the next corner he had to stop. There was a long line of cars ahead of him. They were not moving at all. People were shouting, a man with a black bag hurried past.

"That must be the doctor," Bill thought. He left his car at the side of the road and walked towards the scene of the accident.

Police cars, ambulances, AA patrol cars were parked on both sides of the road. Policemen were keeping back a crowd of people.

"Where's the accident?" Bill asked a boy on a bicycle.

"Look over there!" the boy said.

Bill saw three cars in the ditch and a large lorry on its side in the middle of the road. The lorry driver was sitting on the grass. He was waving his arms angrily and shouting something which Bill could not hear. Three other men were also talking angrily with policemen. The cars did not seem badly damaged, but there were red marks on the road near the lorry.

"How terrible!" Bill said. He looked around him. Two ambulance men were carrying a woman on a stretcher. He tried to get nearer, but a policeman stopped him.

"How many people were killed or injured?" Bill asked excitedly.

"Killed? Injured?" answered the policeman. "Nobody was killed or injured."

"But the woman on the stretcher? The blood?" Bill cried.

"Blood? There isn't any blood. That's paint. The lorry was carrying a load of red paint."

Bill took out his pen and his note-book.

"Are you a newspaperman?" the policeman asked.

"Yes," said Bill.

"Well, you tell your readers that the English love animals too much," the policeman went on. "That woman on the stretcher isn't hurt. Even her car is all right. She's just frightened."

"Frightened?" said Bill. "Frightened of what?"

"She's frightened of the lorry driver and of the drivers of the cars in the ditch. You see, she didn't want to run over a rabbit. She missed the rabbit, but——"

Bill had his story. He began to write in his note-book: "Woman destroys lorry and three cars in order to save rabbit."

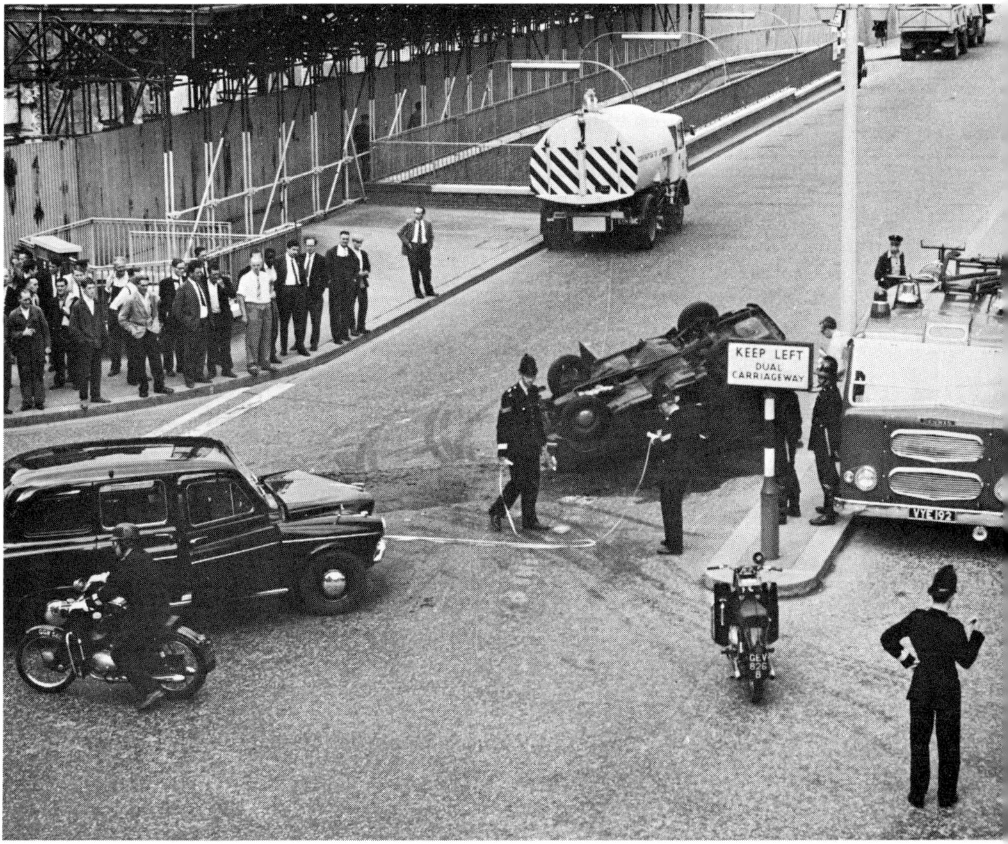


In every country there are more road accidents every year. The Government's Road Research Laboratory tries to find out why accidents happen. Men from the Laboratory take photographs, talk to drivers, and help the Police to make our roads safer. There are new laws to stop drivers using their cars when they have been drinking. These laws have lowered the number of accidents late at night. Another law has made the top speed anywhere in Great Britain 70 miles an hour.

# 4:2 Fire

**bang** /bæŋ/ noise of an explosion (see below). *There was a loud bang, and pieces of the car flew through the air. Please don't bang the door.*

**chief** /tʃiːf/ head (man). *The work of a city fire chief is not easy. The chief clerk looks after all the office work.*

**coal** /kəul/—*Coal* is black, we burn it in fires; we also make gas from coal, and then *coke* is left. *Ordinary coal fires are not allowed in London now.*

**coke** /kəuk/—See *coal* above. *It is hard to light a coke fire, but it burns well, with a hot blue flame.*

**department** /di'pɑːtmənt/ part of a big company (etc.) which does special work; a department store is a very big shop with different departments for men's clothes, women's clothes, books, toys etc. *You'll find record-players in the music department on the third floor, sir.*

**dummy** /'dʌmi/ figure like a person; clothes are shown on *dummies* in shop windows. *Shop window dummies are usually thinner than real people.*

**explosion** /iks'pləuʒn/—When gas suddenly fires with a loud noise, we say it blows up or *explodes*; the loud noise and the rush of gas are an *explosion*. *A bad explosion can kill people.*

**flame** /fleim/ bright parts of burning gas; tongue of fire. *The flames seemed to rush up the stairs.*

**heat** /hiːt/ being hot. *The heat from the burning building drove the crowd back.*

**helmet** /'helmit/ special hat to save the head in dangerous work. *Motor-racing drivers must always wear helmets.*

**hose** /həuz/ long water-pipe that rolls up. *A fire-hose is 75 or 100 feet long.*

**mask** /mɑːsk/ something to go over the face to hide it or to keep smoke or gas out. *Children wear masks at parties. Masked men pointed guns at the people in the bank.*

**paraffin** /'pærəfin/ kind of oil that we use in lamps.

**slip** /slip/ move quickly away by accident. *Be careful not to slip on the wet floor; it's very slippery.*

**upper** /'ʌpə/ near the top. *There is snow on the upper parts of the mountains.*

**just in time** only a moment before something else. *He arrived at 5.59, just in time to catch the 6 o'clock bus.*

## A rather stupid thing

MAN You got here very quickly. Who gave the alarm?

FIREMAN Your neighbour, Mr Potts. You're very lucky to be alive and unhurt, sir.

MAN Is there much damage in the house?

FIREMAN There's a lot of damage in the kitchen—because of the explosion.

MAN The explosion knocked me out. Who saved me?

FIREMAN Mr Potts. He rushed in as soon as he heard the bang. He pulled you into the garden just in time.

MAN What about the rest of the house?

FIREMAN The water has done more damage than the fire. We turned our hoses on the other rooms. We had to do that in order to stop the flames.

MAN I think your men are wonderful. They must be tired. I'm sorry I can't give them all a cup of tea. But the kitchen has gone!

FIREMAN Don't worry about that, sir. Now will you please tell me about the accident. How did it happen? I'll have to make a report.

MAN Well, my wife is away. She's coming back tonight. I was trying to light the old stove in the kitchen.

FIREMAN You mean a stove that burns coal or coke?

MAN That's right.

FIREMAN They're usually quite safe.

MAN Yes, but I did a rather stupid thing—I poured paraffin on it! There was a loud bang. I don't remember anything after that.

---

## Exercise

**1** *Example* He heard the bang, and he rushed in at once.
*Answer* He rushed in as soon as he heard the bang.

1 He saw the fire, and he telephoned the fire-station at once.
2 Bill stepped on the wet floor, and he slipped and fell at once.
3 The firemen arrived, and they ran out their hoses at once.
4 We saw the smoke, and we put our masks on at once.
5 The flames reached the stairs, and the firemen brought their ladders at once.
6 The Fire Chief saw the burning buildings, and he called for help at once.

**2** *Example* We had to stop the fire. We did that.
*Answer* We had to do that in order to stop the fire.

1 They had to fight the fire. They called more fire-engines.
2 The men had to go into the building. They put masks on.
3 You have to save your head. You wear a helmet.
4 They had to put the fire out. They ran out several hoses.
5 He had to buy paraffin. He went to the department store.
6 They had to carry Bill away. They brought a stretcher.

## Bill in danger

The largest department store in the city was on fire. Smoke and flames were coming out of all the upper windows and the roof. Fire-engines were arriving all the time. They were coming from every fire-station in town, and the Fire Chief had already asked for more help. Bill, the reporter from the *Evening Post*, arrived on the scene only a few moments after the first fire-engine.

"Is there anybody inside?" Bill asked a man in the crowd.

"There must be," answered the man. "Look!"

Bill looked. He saw a large number of firemen who were holding hoses. The pumps were shooting thousands of gallons of water into the building. Through the curtain of water Bill saw a ladder. It was rising with great speed from a large red engine near the building. The fireman brought the ladder round to a window just below the roof.

Bill noticed another fireman at the top of the ladder. Suddenly a woman jumped out of the window into the fireman's arms. The fireman put her over his shoulder, and the ladder was brought down to the ground again.

"That woman could tell an exciting story!" Bill thought. He took out his notebook and began to run towards the fire-engine. But the fire had reached the bottom of the building, and a great cloud of smoke was pouring from the broken street windows. Policemen pushed the crowd back, and Bill was suddenly alone in front of the burning building. He was just going to turn back when he saw something through the smoke—a head and an arm. It was the body of a man! It was lying on the floor near the door.

Bill rushed forward. He ran into the burning building, but slipped on the wet floor and fell down. He could not get up. The smoke filled his eyes and his nose. The heat was terrible.

"Is this the end?" he wondered. "Am I going to die?"

At that moment he felt two hands under his arms. And when he looked up he saw the masks and black helmets of two firemen. They lifted him up and carried him into the street.

"Get an ambulance man," one of the firemen said, as they laid him down.

"Don't wait!" Bill whispered. "I'm all right. Go back at once and save that other man."

"What other man?" asked the firemen.

"There was a body," said Bill. "It was lying on the floor near the door."

"Body?" cried one of the firemen. "That wasn't a body! It was a dummy out of the shop window."

There are still too many deaths from fire in the home. Careless parents forget the danger of fire although about 180 children die in this way every year. Posters or notices like this one are shown in many public places.

Factory fires are very dangerous and firemen sometimes lose their lives when they fight them. Many buildings have special fire doors. These are not locked while there are people in the building.

# 4:3 Police

**bottom** /ˈbɔtəm/ lowest part. *There are rocks at the bottom of the sea.*

**CID** (Criminal Investigation Department) /ˈsiːaiˈdiː/ police department which finds out about crime (law-breaking) and criminals (people who break the law). *Another name for a CID man is "detective".*

**dial** /ˈdaiəl/ round instrument on a telephone. *You move the dial to each number in turn. If you want the police, an ambulance or fireman, you dial 999.*

**editor** /ˈeditə/ head of a newspaper office. *The editor decided not to use Bill's story in Monday's newspaper.*

**handcuffs** /ˈhænkʌfs/ iron rings to lock round the wrists (the arms just above the hands). *Sometimes the handcuffs hold a prisoner's two wrists together.*

**licence** /ˈlaisəns/ paper that allows you to use something. *You get a television licence at a post office.*

**one-way street** /ˈwʌnwei ˈstriːt/—Cars etc. cannot go both ways along a *one-way* street. *It is "careless driving" to go the wrong way in a one-way street.*

**phone** /fəun/ telephone. *He rushed to the phone and phoned the police.*

**reverse** /riˈvəːs/ make a car go backwards. *Reverse from a busy road into a side street; don't come out of a side street in reverse.*

**robber** /ˈrɔbə/ man who steals openly, using a gun or his strength etc. *They caught the bank robbers when their car broke down.*

**scream** /skriːm/ loud cry of pain, or a noise like it. *I can't work while the baby is screaming. The scream of car tyres on a corner is frightening.*

**spare** /spɛə/ not in use but ready for use. *Every car has a spare wheel. That garage keeps spares for Volkswagens.*

**tyre** /ˈtaiə/ part of a wheel that touches the road. *The tyres scream when a car corners very fast or stops too suddenly.*

**whistle** /ˈwisl/ small instrument that you blow to make people pay attention to you. *A policeman's whistle is small but it makes a loud noise.*

**go shopping** go out and visit several shops. *Don't go shopping on Saturday mornings if you don't like crowds.*

## A lost key

WOMAN I've come about my car key. I've lost it.
POLICEMAN When did you lose it, madam?
WOMAN I don't know, really. I went into a lot of shops.
POLICEMAN Where is the car now?
WOMAN In the car park round the corner. It's a blue Ford Cortina, and my little dog, Fluff, is locked inside it.
POLICEMAN Where do you usually keep your key?
WOMAN In my handbag.
POLICEMAN Have you looked in all your pockets?
WOMAN Of course.
POLICEMAN Please give me your name and address, madam, and your telephone number. We'll phone you if your other key is found.
WOMAN Mrs Millicent Carruthers, 8 Roseberry Avenue. My telephone number is Billerton 2087.
POLICEMAN Roseberry Avenue? That's not very far. Have you got a spare key?
WOMAN Yes. It's at home.
POLICEMAN Well, then, why don't you go back to Roseberry Avenue and get it?
WOMAN That's a wonderful idea. But I'm afraid I can't get into the house.
POLICEMAN Do you mean that you've lost your front door key too?
WOMAN Oh no! I haven't *lost* it. I always put it in a very safe place when I go shopping. But——
POLICEMAN You mean——?
WOMAN I'm afraid so, officer. It's locked inside the car with Fluff.

---

## Exercise

**1** *Example* I haven't got a front door key. (lose)
*Answer* Do you mean you've lost your front door key?

1 I haven't got a spare tyre. (lose)
2 The phone doesn't work. (break)
3 I haven't brought your van back. (crash)
4 I can't put handcuffs on him. (not bring)
5 I've got another wrong number. (dial)
6 There isn't a one-way street notice. (not see)

**2** *Example* Somebody finds your key. We'll phone you.
*Answer* We'll phone you if your key is found.

1 Somebody wants your story. The editor will phone you.
2 Somebody catches the robbers. He'll tell Bill.
3 Somebody blows the whistle. The policemen will come.
4 Somebody dials 999. There'll be a quick answer.
5 Somebody hurts the child. The child will scream.
6 Somebody robs the bank. Alarms will sound.

## Bank robbers

The editor called Bill to his office. "A man has phoned from a telephone in King Street. He has just seen a bank robbery. He says that he has already dialled 999. So the police are on their way. Get there at once."

Bill ran downstairs and jumped into his car. King Street was on the other side of the town. "If I go up Hammer Hill, it will save five minutes," he thought. Hammer Hill was a one-way street. It was quite narrow but nearly always empty.

Bill drove very fast up the hill. He had reached forty miles an hour when suddenly he heard the scream of tyres. Another car was coming round the corner at the top of the hill. It was a Jaguar. The two cars stopped just in time. Bill said "sorry" to the driver of the Jaguar and began to reverse.

At that moment a policeman blew his whistle and shouted "Stop!" Bill stopped at once. "Can't you see that this is a one-way street?" said the policeman. "You were going the wrong way. Your licence, please."

While the policeman was examining the licence, the Jaguar tried to pass Bill's car. But there was not enough room. "Move, can't you!" shouted the driver. Bill noticed that there were two women with long yellow hair in the back of the car.

The policeman turned to the driver of the Jaguar. "I'm afraid you'll have to wait, too, sir," he said. "I'll want to see *your* licence next. You were driving too fast." The man did not answer. He began to reverse.

At that moment there was a sound of sirens. A black police car stopped at the bottom of the hill, and policemen jumped out. Another police car came round the corner at the top of the hill and crashed into the back of the Jaguar. Four CID men jumped out. They opened the doors of the Jaguar and pulled out the two women. "Are they hurt?" Bill wondered. But they were *not* hurt. In fact they began to fight the policemen.

Suddenly their yellow hair fell off, and Bill saw that they were men. The policemen put handcuffs on them. Then they took them, with the driver, down the street to a police van. Bill was excited. He took out his notebook. One of the CID men walked past. He knew Bill and stopped.

"Thank you, Bill," he said. "This time you'll be able to write a *true* story, won't you? HOW I HELPED TO CATCH THE BANK ROBBERS."

The British policeman is famous for his friendly help. People in difficulties of all kinds often telephone the Police first. But his main job is finding out about crime. As criminals have become more dangerous, the Police have changed too. They now use modern methods of detection. In Liverpool every policeman carries a radio so that he can speak to the Police Station. Information is therefore quickly reported to and from different parts of the city.

Traffic problems still take up much of a policeman's time. Some people think that a special Traffic Police Force for Britain would be a good idea.

# 4:4 The Hospital

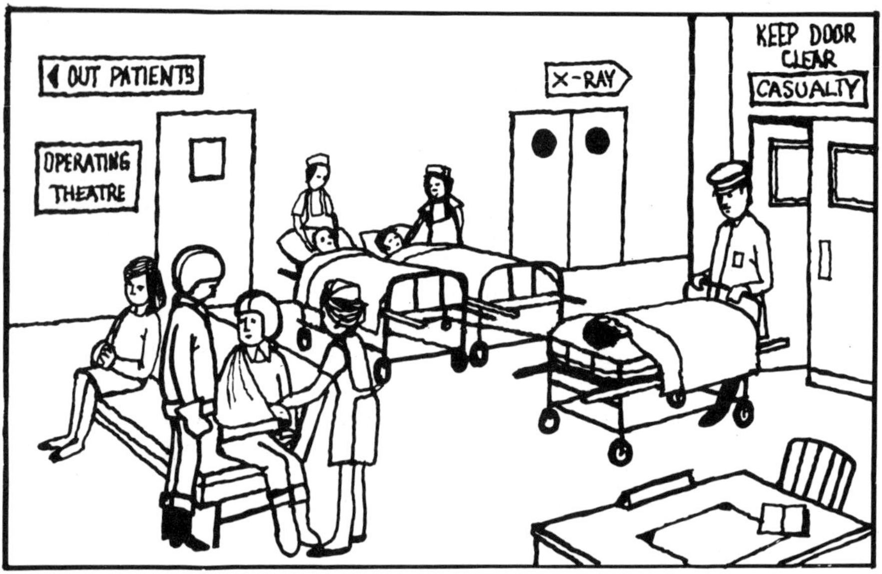


**attend to** /ə'tend tu/ look after; give one's attention to.

**bandage** /'bændidʒ/ long narrow piece of cloth for wounds. *A new bandage comes in a roll. All nurses must be able to bandage a wound.*

**casualty** /'kæzjuəlti/ person who has been hurt in an accident. *After an accident, the patient goes to the casualty department of the hospital.*

**dress** /dres/ clean and bandage (wounds). *"There! I've dressed your wounds and you can go home. Come again tomorrow morning and we'll change the dressings."*

**duty** /'djuːti/ work; a doctor who is *on duty* must be ready to look after patients at any moment. *Dr Smith is on duty until midnight; he's in the doctors' room.*

**groan** /grəun/ sound from a person who is in great pain. *There were groans from several patients. One woman groaned all night.*

**matron** /'meitrən/ woman head of all the sisters and nurses in a hospital.

**motor-bike** /'məutəbaik/ (also motor-cycle) bicycle with an engine. *Your motor-bike is a dangerous machine, isn't it?*

**operate** /'ɔpəreit/ cut into the body to reach a part that is not right. *Mr Jones, the surgeon, is in the operating theatre. He is operating on a man who badly needed the operation.*

**out-patient** /'autpeiʃənt/ person who lives at home and visits the hospital to see a doctor. *Dr Johnson sees out-patients at the hospital from 2.30 to 4.30.*

**patient** /'peiʃənt/ person who is ill and visits a doctor; person who is in hospital. *The new hospital has beds for 400 patients.*

**poison** /'pɔizn/ something that you cannot eat or drink safely; food-poisoning is stomach trouble from bad food. *That man drank poison to end his life.*

**sister** /'sistə/ nurse who is head of the nurses in one part of a hospital. *Keep the patient warm, sister, and change his dressings twice a day.*

**surgeon** /'səːdʒən/ doctor who *operates. Mr Jones is a very good surgeon with a special interest in stomach operations.*

**wheel** /wiːl/ move (something) on wheels.

## "How did you do it?"

NURSE (*opens the door of the Out-Patients' waiting-room*) Will you wait in here, please, Mr Cobley.

WOMAN Are you the Mr Cobley who saved those children on the mountain on Sunday?

COBLEY Well, yes. But it wasn't very difficult, you know.

WOMAN You are brave. I see that your foot is wrapped up in a bandage. Are you going to see the bone surgeon, Mr Harcourt? He's a very nice man. I saw him every Tuesday afternoon last year. He mended my back for me.

COBLEY Really? Are you going to see Mr Harcourt too?

WOMAN Oh no! I'm seeing Doctor Livesey about the pain in my stomach. It's terrible. I can't eat anything at all. I'm sick every night and——

NURSE Mr Cobley, will you come this way, please? Mr Harcourt is ready for you now.

SURGEON Good afternoon, Mr Cobley. I'm very glad to see you. I read about you in the papers yesterday. Splendid! We need brave young men like you.

COBLEY It was nothing, really.

SURGEON Now, Nurse, take off the bandage and let's see this foot. It looks rather nasty. Is it painful?

COBLEY I'm afraid it is. My doctor thinks it's broken.

SURGEON Yes. He says so in his letter to me. Tell me, now, how did you do it? Was it hit by a rock on the mountain?

COBLEY No, it wasn't a rock——

SURGEON Did you slip then? The rocks were wet after all that rain, weren't they?

COBLEY Well, no, I didn't slip. I broke it when I jumped out of bed this morning.

---

## Exercise

**1** *Example* It's got rather a nasty look.
*Answer* It looks rather nasty.

1 It's got rather a nice taste.
2 The dressing has rather a bad smell.
3 The surgeon has rather an angry look.
4 The bandage has rather a wet feel.
5 The matron has rather a busy look.
6 The poison has rather a terrible smell.

**2** *Example* Mr Cobley saved those children.
*Answer* Are you the Mr Cobley who saved those children?

1 Sister Smith works in the operating theatre.
2 Dr Johnson sees the out-patients.
3 Nurse Brown changed the patient's dressing.
4 Mr Jones operated on that patient.
5 Mrs Robinson wanted to see the surgeon.
6 Sister Snow bandaged my son's wounds.

## Phoning for a doctor

Bill was passing through Bilchester when he noticed four ambulances in front of the White Horse Hotel. He stopped at once and took out his notebook. Ambulance men were carrying stretchers into the street, and he could hear groans.

"What has happened?" he asked a girl who was standing near the door.

"They suddenly began to have terrible pains and they were very sick," she said. "I was in the restaurant. I saw it all. It must be food-poisoning."

At that moment the ambulances began to drive off. Bill drove after them to the hospital. While the ambulance men were unloading the stretchers, Bill walked into the Casualty Department. It was full of nurses. But they were all so busy that they took no notice of him. One nurse was dressing the wounds of two boys who had fallen off their motor-bike. In another corner a woman who had burnt her fingers was sitting on a chair and crying.

The ambulance men wheeled the stretchers—ten of them—to the middle of the floor. Nurses began to attend to the new patients. Bill moved nearer.

"Can't we get Doctor Ranji?" asked a nurse.

"No," said the sister. "He's in the operating theatre and the surgeon won't allow him to leave."

"What about Doctor Bradbury?"

"It's his evening off, and he's playing golf. But matron is phoning the two doctors who are on duty in the town."

At that moment the matron came in. "It's no good," she said. "Doctor Scott has gone to a woman who is having a baby. Doctor Burt is out too. There has been an accident with a tractor at the fruit farm. *You* will have to look after the patients until I find another doctor. How are they?"

"I think they're a little better," said the sister. "But they are still asking for a doctor. One of them said, 'Phone Saint Mary's Hospital, Portsmouth.' "

"Good idea!" said the matron. "Put them to bed and keep them warm. Meanwhile I'll phone Portsmouth."

Bill stopped an ambulance man as he was leaving. "Tell me," he said. "Why is the matron phoning Portsmouth?"

The ambulance man looked at him with surprise. "Didn't you hear?" he said. "We need a doctor. The two young doctors who live in the hospital aren't here. The other two doctors——"

"Do you mean that there are only *four* doctors in this town?" Bill asked.

"Of course not! We've got a *lot* of doctors," said the ambulance man proudly.

"But where are all the rest of them?" cried Bill.

"Well, you see, our Doctor Cameron was 80 years old today. So the other doctors decided to give him a party—at the White Horse. They asked for a very special fish dish. Now they're all on those stretchers!"

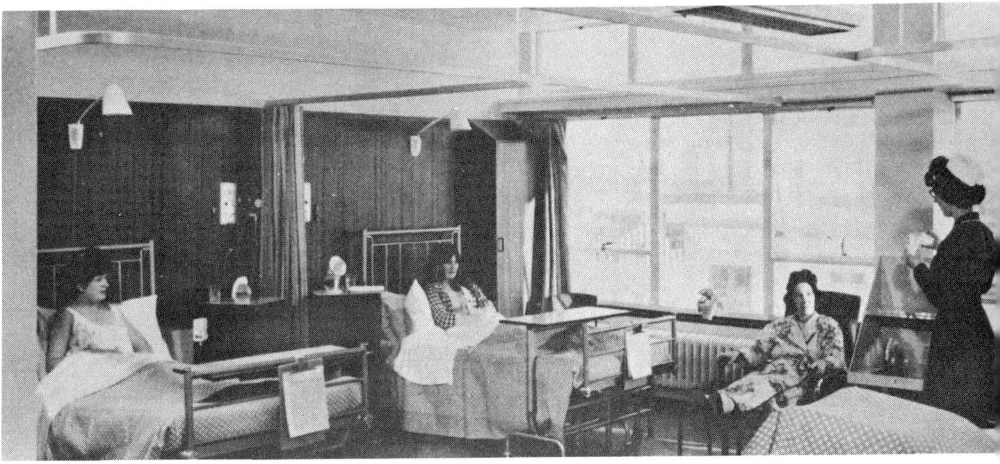

In the top picture you can see a modern hospital in the new town of Harlow. It is in the centre of the town near the shops but there are trees and gardens round it. New hospitals have four to six patients in a ward. Some old hospitals have about twenty patients in a ward.

The other picture shows an operation in a teaching hospital. You can see the students watching the operation. The surgeon is talking to the students. Opposite the surgeon is the sister who hands him the instruments.

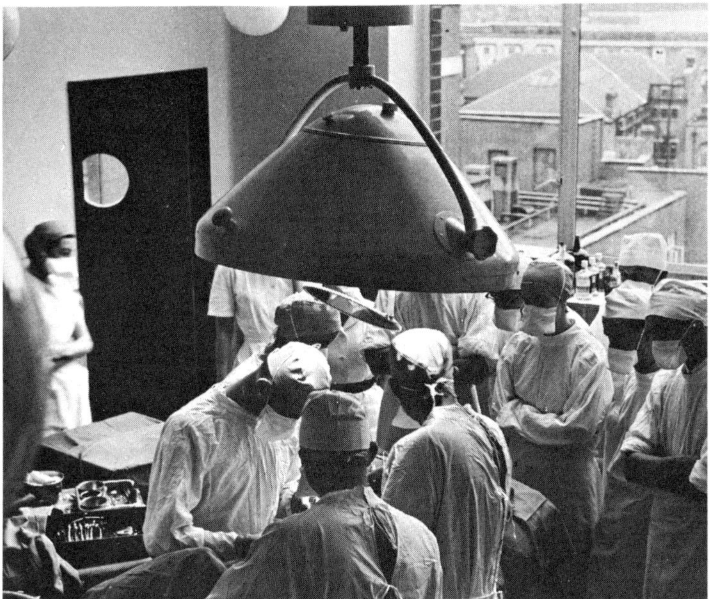

# 4:5 Travelling

**afford** /əˈfɔːd/ be able to pay for (something). *"Our coffee has gone up to twice the price. Can we afford it?" We can't afford to buy a new car.*

**carriage** /ˈkæridʒ/ separate part of a train, with seats for about eighty passengers. *A carriage is sometimes divided into compartments. I never travel in the last carriage of a train.*

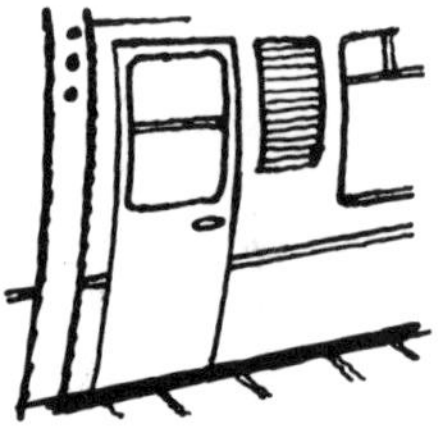

**change** /tʃeindʒ/ money that somebody (a shopkeeper etc.) returns to us. *I gave you a £5 note and you have given me change for only £1.*

**communication cord** /kəmjuːniˈkeiʃn kɔːd/—If there is danger, we can pull the communication cord; when we pull it, the train stops. *We pulled the communication cord when there was no danger, and it cost us £25.*

**compartment** /kəmˈpɑːtmənt/ part of a carriage. *A compartment has seats for six (1st class), eight or ten passengers.*

**conductress** /kənˈdʌktris/ woman who looks after bus passengers, sells tickets etc.; *a conductor* is a man who does that.

**fare** /fɛə/ cost of a ticket. *Fares, please! Any more fares, please? The fare from here to Waterloo is 5p.*

**guard** /gɑːd/ man who looks after a train and its passengers. *The guard has a lamp, a whistle, a green flag and a red flag.*

**non-smoking** /ˈnɔnˈsməukiŋ/ not for people who want to smoke. *The red sign "NO SMOKING" means that you must not smoke in that part of the train.*

**platform** /ˈplætfɔːm/ long raised part beside the lines in a station; you step into a train from the platform. *London's Victoria Station has seventeen platforms. A bus conductress stands on the platform at the back of the bus.*

**rush hour** /ˈrʌʃ auə/ time when most people go to work (8–9) or go home (5–6). *Try not to travel in the rush hour. Rush-hour traffic in our big cities is terrible.*

**thief** /θiːf/ criminal who steals. *Thieves broke into the shop last night and stole some money.*

## "Move along, please!"

CONDUCTRESS Any more fares, please?

OLD LADY I want to go to Piccadilly Circus.

CONDUCTRESS You're going the wrong way, dear. You'll have to get off at the next stop. Cross the street and take a number 3 bus. (*To another passenger*) I haven't got the right change, sir. I'm afraid you'll have to wait.

YOUNG MAN (*to girl-friend*) There's one seat up at the front. (*to conductress*) Can I stand?

CONDUCTRESS You can stand, yes. But you'll have to put away your pipe. Smoking is not allowed downstairs. If you want to smoke you'll have to go on top.

YOUNG MAN (*to girl-friend*) Come on. Let's go upstairs.

CONDUCTRESS (*to man with large case*) Leave your case under the stairs, sir. There's no room for it in here. Move along, please!

OLD MAN Can I get off here?

CONDUCTRESS Not really, sir. It would be dangerous. We're at traffic lights.

OLD MAN Oh dear! I'm afraid of all these cars and buses. There's too much traffic in London today.

CONDUCTRESS (*goes upstairs and sees the young man. He is standing beside his girl-friend and is smoking.*) I'm sorry, but you can't stay here.

YOUNG MAN But you said that I could smoke upstairs.

CONDUCTRESS Yes, sir, that's quite right. You can *smoke*, but you are not allowed to *stand*.

---

## Exercise

**1** *Example* Do not smoke downstairs.
*Answer* Smoking is not allowed downstairs.

1 Do not stand upstairs.
2 Do not smoke in this compartment.
3 Do not turn right at these traffic lights.
4 Do not stop in this street in the rush hour.
5 Do not park near a cross-roads.
6 Do not swim in the Regent's Park lake.

**2** *Example* What about London today? (traffic)
*Answer* There's too much traffic in London today.

1 What about the conductress's bag? (change)
2 What about rush-hour trains? (too many passengers on)
3 What about the corridor? (people)
4 What about this compartment? (smoke)
5 What about the station platform? (passengers)
6 What about the Casualty Department? (work)

## The man in black

It was the rush hour and Bill was on his way home from London. When he reached Waterloo station the train was already standing at the platform. Nearly all the carriages were full, but Bill found a seat between two fat ladies in a non-smoking compartment.

The guard blew his whistle. Just then a man ran down the platform, opened the carriage door and jumped into the compartment. He was wearing a black hat and a black suit, and he was carrying a black bag, an umbrella and an evening newspaper. He pushed past the ladies' legs, opened the door into the corridor and walked towards the front of the train.

"What a nasty man!" said one of the fat ladies. "He didn't even say 'Excuse me'."

The train did not stop until it reached the country. Then it stopped at every station. Nearly all the passengers got out—except the two ladies in Bill's compartment. They were talking all the time. They talked so loudly that at last Bill got up and went into the corridor. But he could hear them even there. So he began to walk down the train.

He had almost reached the front carriage when suddenly he saw the man in black again. He was standing at the open window of a first-class compartment. His right hand was holding the communication cord! He was quite alone in the compartment.

"Where's my notebook?" Bill thought. "There's a story here."

But before he could do anything, the man pulled the cord. The train stopped so quickly that Bill fell forward. When he got up the man had gone. He rushed to the window. The man in black was walking quickly towards a large house in the middle of a park. Bill was just going to jump down and run after him, when the guard arrived. The guard looked angrily at Bill.

"Who pulled the cord?" he asked.

Bill was very excited. He pointed.

"It was that man!" he cried. "The one who is walking towards that big house. I think he's a thief. I'll run to the house while you phone the police."

The guard looked out of the window.

"Thief, did you say?" he said. "That's Sir Bertram Montague. He sometimes doesn't get out at the station—he pulls the communication cord as the train passes his house. It costs him £25 each time. But he's so rich that he can afford it."

London's traffic problems are not new, and they are growing greater every year. The new Victoria Line, a modern underground railway, will help people to get to work more quickly. Because of the crowded roads, buses move slowly in the rush hours, and passengers become discouraged and angry. There are plans for two new roads round London—the Inner Box and the Outer Box. These roads will help traffic move more freely.

# 4:6 Hotels

**actress** /'æktris/ woman who plays parts in the theatre or on films, TV etc. *Which film actress do you like best?*

**bar** /bɑː/ high narrow table for drinks, or the room that it is in. *He's in the bar, having a drink. Shall we sit at a table or stand at the bar?*

**desk** /desk/ table to write at; place in a hotel, airport etc. to talk to the receptionist (see below). *The desks in this school are too small.*

**include** /in'kluːd/ have as a part. *The price of the silver knives and forks includes the leather case.*

**journey** /'dʒəːni/ travel from A to B. *The journey from London to Edinburgh by road takes eight hours.*

**lift** /lift/ electric car that takes people up and down between the floors of a building. *"Lift" is the English word, but Americans call it an "elevator"*

**lounge** /laundʒ/ large room with arm-chairs, sitting-room of a hotel etc. *After dinner we went to the lounge for coffee.*

**luggage** /'lʌgidʒ/ traveller's bags, cases etc. *The porter will take your luggage to the train.*

**page** /peidʒ/ boy who works in an hotel etc. *A page calls your name in the lounge, bars etc. when your guest arrives. Ask a page to bring you some cigarettes.*

**porter** /'pɔːtə/ man who looks after bags and cases in hotels, on stations etc. *The porter will order a taxi for you.*

**receptionist** /ri'sepʃənist/ person (usually a girl) who receives you at an hotel etc. *I signed the visitor's book at the reception desk, and the receptionist gave me my key.*

**tip** /tip/ present of money for a porter, hotel servant etc. *Some hotels add ten per cent to the bill and do not allow hotel servants to accept tips.*

**trainer** /'treinə/ person who helps another person to prepare for a sport (running races, boxing, rowing etc.). *An Olympic runner's trainer has usually been a runner, but the trainer of a racehorse was never a horse.*

**all right** *You'll be all right* = You will feel better.

**matter** *That doesn't matter* = You do not need to worry about that.

## A family arrives

HUSBAND My wife and I would like a double room, and I want two single rooms for my son and daughter.

RECEPTIONIST Just for tonight, sir?

HUSBAND Yes. Have you got a double room with a shower?

RECEPTIONIST No, sir. But I've got a large double room with a bathroom.

HUSBAND How much is that?

RECEPTIONIST £5. The price includes breakfast, of course.

HUSBAND What about the single rooms?

RECEPTIONIST I've only got two free—at £3, and they're on different floors.

HUSBAND That doesn't matter. We'll take them, and also the room with the bathroom.

RECEPTIONIST Would you like dinner, sir?

WIFE Oh yes! I'm very hungry. What time is dinner?

RECEPTIONIST We serve dinner from 7.30, madam. Have you got a car? The garage is behind the hotel.

HUSBAND No. We've just come from the station in a taxi. Where is the telephone? Oh yes, there's the box. (*To wife*) Give me 2p, dear. (*He goes to the box.*)

WIFE (*to receptionist*) We've had a terrible journey. Travelling makes me very tired.

RECEPTIONIST I can understand that, madam. But after you've had a good meal, you'll feel all right. The porter will take your cases to your room. Where is your luggage?

WIFE Well, I *hope* it's at the next station. My husband is phoning to find out. You see—we left it on the train.

---

## Exercise

**1** *Example* I get very tired when I travel.
*Answer* Travelling makes me very tired.

1 You get very thirsty when you talk.
2 The porter gets very hungry when he carries luggage.
3 An actress is very happy when she works.
4 The receptionist is very pretty when she makes up her face.
5 The surgeon gets very anxious when he operates.
6 The sister feels very sad when she bandages wounds.

**2** *Example* A good meal will make you feel all right.
*Answer* After you've had a good meal, you'll feel all right.

1 A long sleep will make you feel better.
2 An orange drink in the bar will make you feel fine.
3 A rest in the lounge will make the actress feel all right.
4 A long journey will make you feel tired.
5 A few days in bed will make the patient feel better.
6 A day behind the reception desk will make the new receptionist feel tired.

## "Can I help you?"

"Get down to the Palace Hotel at once," the editor said to Bill. "Lynn Williams is in town."

The Palace Hotel was the only large and expensive hotel in the city. It had fifty bedrooms, a dance hall, a very modern restaurant and two bars.

"I hope that Lynn will invite me into the bar," Bill thought.

Lynn Williams was a Welsh actress. She had just got married but still used her own name. Bill went up to the reception desk. The receptionist was very busy. New arrivals were asking for rooms. Guests who were leaving were paying their bills. Others were just returning their keys. As soon as the receptionist was free, she turned to Bill and said, "Can I help you, sir?"

"I'd like to see Lynn Williams," Bill said. "I'm a newspaper man."

The receptionist looked at her book.

"Room 44," she said. "But I'd better find out——"

At that moment the telephone rang.

"Excuse me, sir," she said to Bill. "Will you please take a seat in the lounge. I'll call you in a minute."

Bill had just sat down, when a page boy came up to him and said, "Mr Blogg is waiting for you at the desk, sir. He will take you up to the room now."

"That must be Lynn's husband," Bill thought. "Blogg! It's a terrible name! I can understand why she has kept her *own* name."

When he reached the reception desk he got an even bigger surprise. Mr Blogg was about fifty. He had a broken nose and he had lost two teeth. He came forward at once and held out his hand to Bill. "You're a newspaper man?" he said. "Lynn will be very glad to see you."

"Thank you, Mr Blogg," Bill said. "Are you—er—Lynn's husband?"

Mr Blogg looked at Bill. His mouth opened, and then he began to laugh. He laughed so much that Bill got angry.

"I'm sorry," Mr Blogg said at last. "Come up in the lift and I'll introduce you to my *wife*." Then he began to laugh again. He laughed while they went up in the lift to the fourth floor. He laughed as they walked along the corridor. He laughed as he opened the door of room 44.

"Lynn!" shouted Mr Blogg. "Here's the newspaper man."

The bathroom door opened, and a very large and very ugly man came out. He was wearing a pair of cotton shorts.

"Meet Lynn!" Mr Blogg said to Bill. "He's the best weight-lifter in Wales, and I'm his trainer."

This hotel in Sussex was built in 1450. A large number of hotels in Great Britain are hundreds of years old. They are usually new inside, but they keep the old wood and their large fireplaces.

The old hotels, often called "inns", are usually in the country. In the big cities visitors can stay at very new hotels. These new hotels are like most modern hotels in other countries.

# 4:7 Money Matters

**account** /ə'kaunt/ record of money. *When a bank looks after your money, you have an account at that bank.*

**cash** /kæʃ/ money in notes, silver etc. not cheques. *Will you take a cheque, or must I pay cash? Will you cash this cheque, please?*

**cheque** /tʃek/ an order to pay money. *You paid me by cheque, but your bank won't give me the money—you forgot to sign your cheque.*

**counter** /'kauntə/ long table in an office or shop. *A post office clerk stands behind the counter to serve people.*

**deposit** /di'pɔzit/ put money into a bank or savings account. *He has deposited £5 to open an account, and he wants to make deposits of £1 a week.*

**matter** /'mætə/ something to decide; *money matters* are decisions about the use of money *My husband looks after all money matters.*

**queue** /kju:/ line of people waiting. *The person who arrives last stands at the end of the queue. Please queue here for the No. 13 bus.*

**savings** /'seiviŋz/ money that you do not spend. *You can put your savings in an old sock, or in the bank, or in a National Savings Account at the Post Office.*

**savings book** /'seiviŋz buk/ small book which shows money going into (*deposits*) and coming out of (*withdrawals*) your National Savings Account. *If you take your Savings Book to any post office you can withdraw money from your account.*

**share** /ʃɛə/ divide between two or more people. *Share this cake among you. Don't take more than your share.*

**signature** /'signətʃə/ person's own name written by himself. *That's not my signature; it isn't one of my cheques either.*

**traveller's cheque** /'trævləz tʃek/ cheque that a traveller can change at any bank. *You can take only £25 out of the country in cash; take the rest in traveller's cheques.*

**withdraw** /wið'drɔ:/ take (money) out. *I want to withdraw £20 from my account.*

**Let's have** = Please give me—or: Please show me.

## A traveller's cheque

WOMAN Here's a traveller's cheque for £20. Will you please change it for me.

BANK CLERK You must sign first, madam.

WOMAN But it's already signed at the top.

BANK CLERK I know, but before I give you the money, you must sign again at the bottom.

WOMAN Oh dear! I'm afraid I don't understand about traveller's cheques. I've never used them before.

BANK CLERK Didn't your bank explain to you what to do?

WOMAN Oh no! My husband looks after money matters in our family.

BANK CLERK When you buy the cheques, you sign them at the top. When you want to cash them, you sign them again at the bottom.

WOMAN Oh, I see! That's very easy.

BANK CLERK (*looks at her signature*) You're Mrs Roberts?

WOMAN Of course I am! Look! I've signed—Barbara Roberts.

BANK CLERK But madam, this signature is quite different from the signature at the top.

WOMAN Of course it is! That's my husband's signature. Can't I sign for him? We always share our money.

BANK CLERK I'm very sorry, madam. The signature at the top must be exactly the same as the signature at the bottom.

WOMAN Oh dear! I've seen a lovely evening dress in the shop round the corner. But I'll never make my husband sign. You see, we're camping.

---

## Exercise

**1** *Example* My husband will never sign. (I)
*Answer* I'll never make my husband sign.

1 My brother will never stand in a queue. (Nobody)
2 The old woman will never open a Savings Account. (Her son)
3 He'll never use a cheque. (You)
4 The bank clerk will never cash this traveller's cheque. (Nothing)
5 He'll never remember to bring his Savings Book. (We)
6 That chap will never pay his share. (His friends)

**2** *Example* We can't do anything. He never explained.
*Answer* Didn't he explain to you what to do?

1 We can't say anything. He never told us.
2 I can't buy anything. She never told me.
3 She can't write anything. The cashier never explained.
4 I can't eat anything. The surgeon never told me.
5 She can't bandage anything. The surgeon didn't explain.
6 I can't withdraw anything. My husband didn't tell me.

## Post Office Savings

Bill had gone to the post office for some stamps. It was the end of the week and there was a long queue at the counter. The woman in front of Bill was talking angrily to the clerk about her National Savings account.

"I'm sorry, madam," the clerk said. "I can't give you £50."

"Why not? I've got £500 in my account!" cried the woman. "I deposited £100 last week."

"I know, madam," the clerk said. "But I've already told you, if you want to withdraw more than £20 you must give us four days' warning. Please fill in this form."

The woman picked up the form and took it away. Bill bought his stamps. He was just going to leave when he noticed a very small boy. The child was standing in the middle of the queue. He was very dirty, and his trousers and his shirt were wet.

"What *are* you doing in here?" a woman said to the child. "Go home at once and change your clothes."

The little boy did not say anything until he reached the counter. Then he said, very slowly and very carefully, "I want to open a Savings Account."

Everybody laughed.

"Let's have your pennies, then," said the clerk.

"I haven't got any pennies," said the little boy. "I've only got this piece of paper." He handed to the clerk a piece of blue paper. There were dirty marks on it, and one of the corners was off. But when the clerk held it up, there was a cry of surprise. It was a £5 note.

"Where did you find this, son?" the clerk asked.

"An old lady gave it to me, because I pulled her dog out of the lake," the boy said. " 'Take it to the post office,' she said, 'and open a Savings Account.' What is a Savings Account?"

"How old are you?" asked the clerk.

"I'm seven today," the little boy answered.

"Then you're just old enough," the clerk said. "You *can* put your money in the National Savings Bank." He gave the little boy a special form and a Savings Book. Then he showed him the places where he had to sign.

When the little boy walked out of the post office, Bill ran after him. "Did you say that you were seven years old *today*?" Bill asked.

"Yes," said the little boy, and walked on. Bill took out his notebook and began to write, "England's youngest saver opens National Savings Account."

At that moment the little boy turned and came back to Bill. "Please could you give me 2p," he said. "I want to go home and I haven't got any money for the bus."

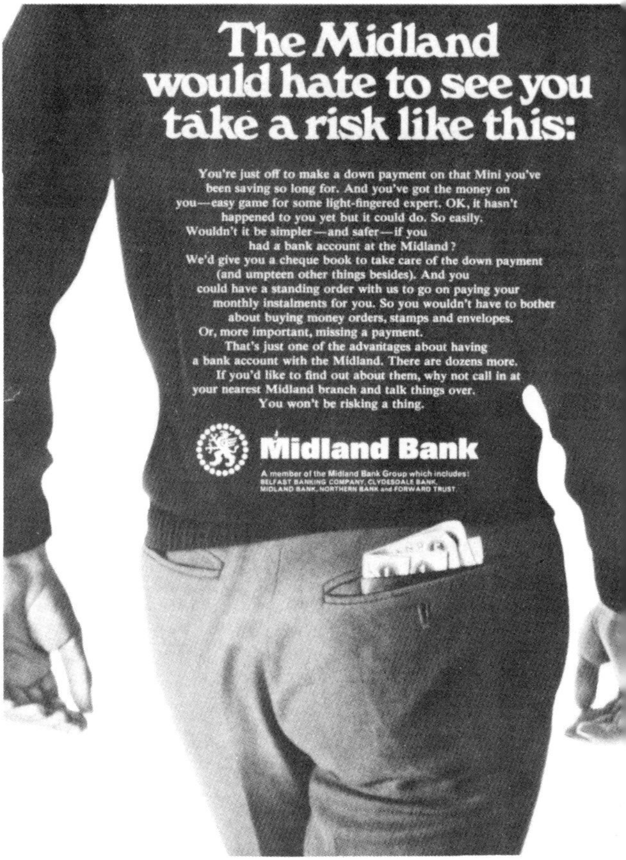


There is no need to buy things with cash today; all large shops will accept cheques. Banks and Post Offices are giving new services. The Trafalgar Square Post Office in London is open all night. As you can see from the picture it is a large, modern building.

# Arrival in Britain

**VOM INHABER VOR DER ANKUNFT IM VEREINIGTEN KÖNIGREICH AUSZUFÜLLEN**
**TO BE COMPLETED BY THE HOLDER BEFORE ARRIVAL IN THE UNITED KINGDOM**

**Familienname** ....MUELLER....
Family name (BLOCKSCHRIFT) (IN BLOCK LETTERS)

**Vornamen** ....Franz....
First names

**Staatsangehörigkeit** ....German....
Nationality

**Nummer des nationalen Personalausweises**..123/45/678
Serial Number of National Identity Card

**Unterschrift des Inhabers** ....Franz Müller....
Holder's signature

**Name und Alter von begleitenden Kindern unter 16 Jahren**
Name and ages of accompanying children under 16 years of age

| Name | Alter |
|---|---|
| Jürgen Müller | 12 |
| | |
| | |
| | |

2

**Für amtliche Eintragungen im Vereinigten Königreich**
For official use in the United Kingdom

**EINREISEBEDINGUNGEN**
Landing Conditions

VISIT UP TO THREE MONTHS
IMMIGRATION OFFICER
16 JUN 1962
DOVER

IMMIGRATION OFFICER
- 7 JUL 1962
DOVER

---

**EMBARKATION CARD** **ALIENS ORDER, 1953** **IB 29A**

Port of disembarkation ....Dover....

Surname (in block letters) / Nom en caracteres gros / Familienname in Druckschrift / Cognome in Stampato: BARGELLINI

Forenames / Prénoms / Vornamen / Nomi: Alberto

Date of Birth / Date de naissance / Geburtsdatum / Data di nascita: 3.5.1952
Place of birth / Lieu de naissance / Geburtsort / Luogo di nascita: Verona
Sex / Sexe / Geschlecht / Sesso: Male

Nationality / Nationalité / Staatsangehörigkeit / Nazionalità: Italian
Occupation / Profession / Beruf / Professione: University Student

Number of Passport / Numéro du passeport / Passnummer / Numero del passaporto (or, if a national identity card is used in lieu of a passport, number of national identity card): 123/45/678

Full address in United Kingdom / Adresse précise en Grande Bretagne / Genaue Adresse in Grossbritannien / Indirizzo presso in Gran Bretagna:
c/o Mrs. B. Springer,
6, Wellington Avenue, London, N.6.

Signature / Signature / Unterschrift / Firma: Alberto Bargellini

T.113(2nd)

# British Money Old and New

introduced
14 October
1969

withdrawn
15 February
1971

introduced
23 April
1968

not to be
withdrawn

introduced
23 April
1968

not to be
withdrawn

may possibly
be withdrawn
in 1973

introduced
15 February
1971

equal to
4·8d

withdrawn
after 15
February
1971

introduced
15 February
1971

equal to
2·4d

introduced
15 February
1971

equal to
1·2d

withdrawn
after 15
February
1971

# Using a public telephone

Have some—coins (2p or 10p) ready.
Lift the receiver and listen for the dialling tone. It is a low "brrr..." without a break.
Then dial the number that you want.
If you hear a fast "pip-pip-pip ..." on a high note, press in a coin or coins. Then speak. The "pip-pip-pip..." (the pay tone) may begin again while you are speaking. Press in more coins.

**Number engaged:** If the other person's telephone is in use, you will hear a single high note. It comes again and again, slowly.

**Operator:** If you need help, dial 100. The operator will answer.

**Emergency calls:** In an emergency, dial 999. Ask the operator for "Fire" or "Police" or "Ambulance".

**Telephone directories:** The directory gives a list of the names, addresses, and telephone numbers of people in the area.

**Dialling instructions:** A call to a number which is outside the area is a **trunk call**. If you want to make a trunk call, look in the small book called "Dialling Instructions".

**S.T.D. (Subscriber Trunk Dialling):** "S.T.D." means that you can dial trunk calls without the operator's help. Find the S.T.D. code number in "Dialling Instructions", and dial that number first.

All telephone codes are now figures only, and not letters.

**area** /'ɛəriə/ part of the country.

**code** /kəud/ a number for the area.
Example: *My telephone number is 302; my friends in the village just dial 302; but my friends in London dial 04-3774-302. The 04-3774 is the code.*

**coin** /kɔin/ a piece of money (not paper).

**dial** /'daiəl/ (to turn) a ring with finger holes and numbers on a telephone.

**directory** /di'rektəri/ (See above.)

**emergency** /i'məːdʒənsi/ a need for very quick help.

**engaged:** /in'geidʒd/ (See above.)

**operator:** /'ɔpəreitə/ (See above.)

**S.T.D.:** /'es'tiː'diː/ (See above.)

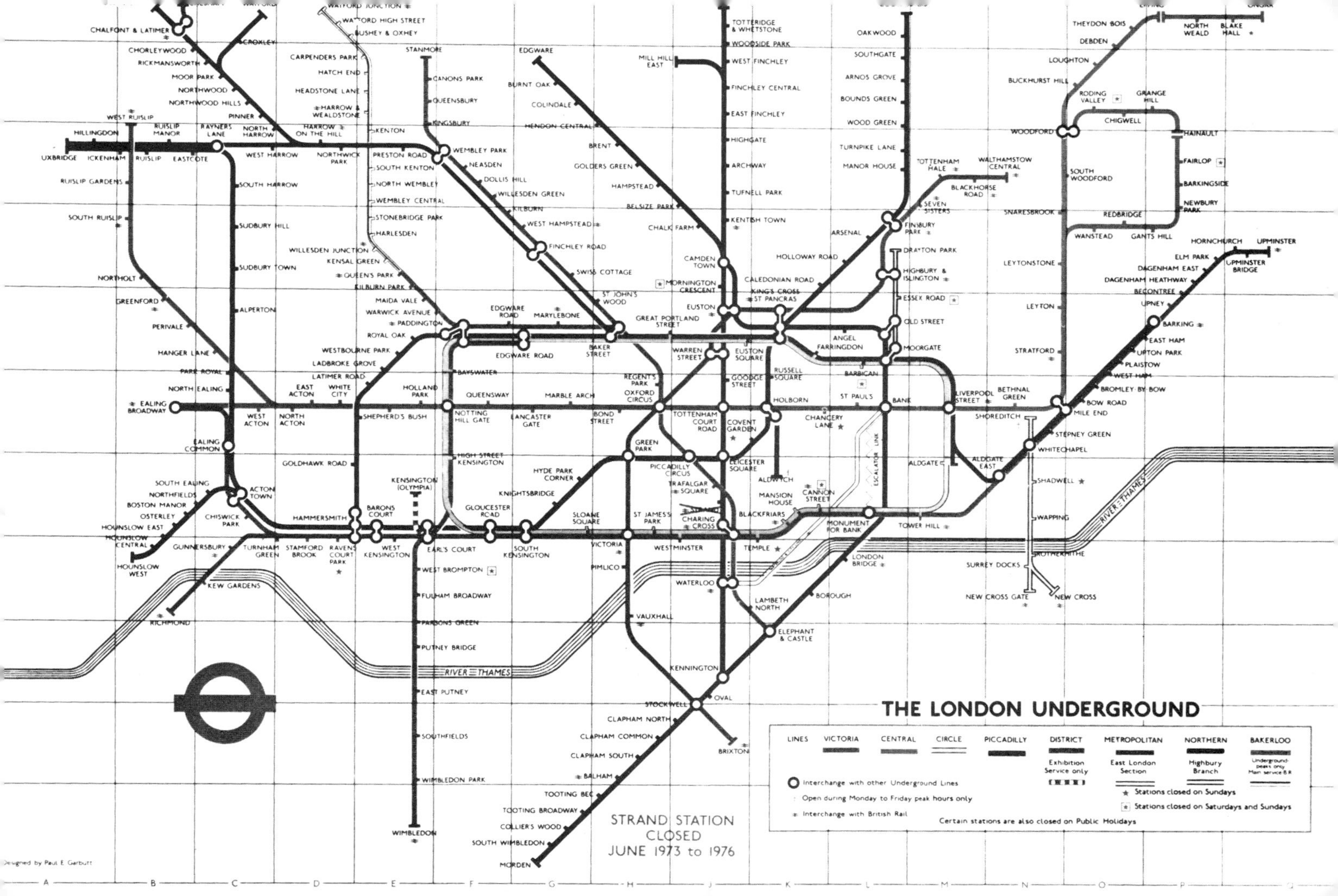
THE LONDON UNDERGROUND
LINES
VICTORIA
CENTRAL
CIRCLE
PICCADILLY
DISTRICT
Exhibition Service only
METROPOLITAN
East London Section
NORTHERN
Highbury Branch
BAKERLOO
Underground: peaks only Main service B.R.
Interchange with other Underground Lines
Open during Monday to Friday peak hours only
Interchange with British Rail
Stations closed on Sundays
Stations closed on Saturdays and Sundays
Certain stations are also closed on Public Holidays
STRAND STATION CLOSED JUNE 1973 to 1976
RIVER THAMES
ESCALATOR LINK
Designed by Paul E. Garbutt
CHALFONT & LATIMER
CHORLEYWOOD
RICKMANSWORTH
CROXLEY
MOOR PARK
NORTHWOOD
NORTHWOOD HILLS
PINNER
NORTH HARROW
HARROW ON THE HILL
WEST HARROW
WATFORD JUNCTION
WATFORD HIGH STREET
BUSHEY & OXHEY
CARPENDERS PARK
HATCH END
HEADSTONE LANE
HARROW & WEALDSTONE
KENTON
STANMORE
CANONS PARK
QUEENSBURY
KINGSBURY
WEST RUISLIP
HILLINGDON
UXBRIDGE
ICKENHAM
RUISLIP
RUISLIP MANOR
EASTCOTE
RAYNERS LANE
RUISLIP GARDENS
SOUTH RUISLIP
NORTHOLT
GREENFORD
PERIVALE
HANGER LANE
SOUTH HARROW
SUDBURY HILL
SUDBURY TOWN
ALPERTON
PARK ROYAL
NORTH EALING
EALING BROADWAY
EALING COMMON
WEST ACTON
NORTH ACTON
EAST ACTON
WHITE CITY
NORTHWICK PARK
PRESTON ROAD
WEMBLEY PARK
SOUTH KENTON
NORTH WEMBLEY
WEMBLEY CENTRAL
STONEBRIDGE PARK
HARLESDEN
WILLESDEN JUNCTION
KENSAL GREEN
QUEENS PARK
KILBURN PARK
MAIDA VALE
WARWICK AVENUE
PADDINGTON
ROYAL OAK
WESTBOURNE PARK
LADBROKE GROVE
LATIMER ROAD
SHEPHERD'S BUSH
HOLLAND PARK
GOLDHAWK ROAD
NEASDEN
DOLLIS HILL
WILLESDEN GREEN
KILBURN
WEST HAMPSTEAD
FINCHLEY ROAD
SWISS COTTAGE
ST JOHN'S WOOD
EDGWARE
BURNT OAK
COLINDALE
HENDON CENTRAL
BRENT
GOLDERS GREEN
HAMPSTEAD
BELSIZE PARK
CHALK FARM
MILL HILL EAST
TOTTERIDGE & WHETSTONE
WOODSIDE PARK
WEST FINCHLEY
FINCHLEY CENTRAL
EAST FINCHLEY
HIGHGATE
ARCHWAY
TUFNELL PARK
KENTISH TOWN
CAMDEN TOWN
MORNINGTON CRESCENT
EUSTON
GREAT PORTLAND STREET
EDGWARE ROAD
MARYLEBONE
BAKER STREET
BAYSWATER
QUEENSWAY
NOTTING HILL GATE
HIGH STREET KENSINGTON
KENSINGTON (OLYMPIA)
LANCASTER GATE
MARBLE ARCH
BOND STREET
REGENT'S PARK
OXFORD CIRCUS
WARREN STREET
EUSTON SQUARE
GOODGE STREET
TOTTENHAM COURT ROAD
COVENT GARDEN
HOLBORN
RUSSELL SQUARE
CHANCERY LANE
ST PAUL'S
BARBICAN
FARRINGDON
ANGEL
KING'S CROSS ST PANCRAS
CALEDONIAN ROAD
HOLLOWAY ROAD
ARSENAL
OAKWOOD
SOUTHGATE
ARNOS GROVE
BOUNDS GREEN
WOOD GREEN
TURNPIKE LANE
MANOR HOUSE
FINSBURY PARK
SEVEN SISTERS
TOTTENHAM HALE
BLACKHORSE ROAD
WALTHAMSTOW CENTRAL
DRAYTON PARK
HIGHBURY & ISLINGTON
ESSEX ROAD
OLD STREET
MOORGATE
BANK
LIVERPOOL STREET
BETHNAL GREEN
SHOREDITCH
ALDGATE
ALDGATE EAST
MILE END
STEPNEY GREEN
WHITECHAPEL
SHADWELL
WAPPING
ROTHERHITHE
SURREY DOCKS
NEW CROSS GATE
NEW CROSS
TOWER HILL
MONUMENT FOR BANK
CANNON STREET
MANSION HOUSE
BLACKFRIARS
ALDWYCH
TEMPLE
EMBANKMENT
CHARING CROSS
TRAFALGAR SQUARE
LEICESTER SQUARE
PICCADILLY CIRCUS
GREEN PARK
HYDE PARK CORNER
KNIGHTSBRIDGE
SOUTH KENSINGTON
GLOUCESTER ROAD
SLOANE SQUARE
ST JAMES'S PARK
WESTMINSTER
VICTORIA
PIMLICO
VAUXHALL
WATERLOO
LAMBETH NORTH
ELEPHANT & CASTLE
BOROUGH
LONDON BRIDGE
KENNINGTON
OVAL
STOCKWELL
BRIXTON
CLAPHAM NORTH
CLAPHAM COMMON
CLAPHAM SOUTH
BALHAM
TOOTING BEC
TOOTING BROADWAY
COLLIER'S WOOD
SOUTH WIMBLEDON
MORDEN
EARL'S COURT
WEST BROMPTON
FULHAM BROADWAY
PARSONS GREEN
PUTNEY BRIDGE
EAST PUTNEY
SOUTHFIELDS
WIMBLEDON PARK
WIMBLEDON
WEST KENSINGTON
BARONS COURT
HAMMERSMITH
RAVENSCOURT PARK
STAMFORD BROOK
TURNHAM GREEN
CHISWICK PARK
ACTON TOWN
SOUTH EALING
NORTHFIELDS
BOSTON MANOR
OSTERLEY
HOUNSLOW EAST
HOUNSLOW CENTRAL
HOUNSLOW WEST
GUNNERSBURY
KEW GARDENS
RICHMOND
THEYDON BOIS
DEBDEN
LOUGHTON
BUCKHURST HILL
NORTH WEALD
BLAKE HALL
RODING VALLEY
GRANGE HILL
CHIGWELL
HAINAULT
FAIRLOP
BARKINGSIDE
NEWBURY PARK
WOODFORD
SOUTH WOODFORD
SNARESBROOK
REDBRIDGE
WANSTEAD
GANTS HILL
LEYTONSTONE
LEYTON
STRATFORD
HORNCHURCH
UPMINSTER
UPMINSTER BRIDGE
ELM PARK
DAGENHAM EAST
DAGENHAM HEATHWAY
BECONTREE
UPNEY
BARKING
EAST HAM
UPTON PARK
PLAISTOW
WEST HAM
BROMLEY BY BOW
BOW ROAD
A
B
C
D
E
F
G
H
J
K
L
M
N
O
P